Lessons from the Legends

LESSONS
FROM THE
LEGENDS

**NEW APPLICATIONS FROM THE
TIMELESS WISDOM OF
JOHN WOODEN
& PAT SUMMITT**

BRIAN BIRO

NEW YORK

LONDON • NASHVILLE • MELBOURNE • VANCOUVER

Lessons from the Legends

New Applications from the Timeless Wisdom of John Wooden and Pat Summitt

Published in New York, New York, by Morgan James Publishing. Morgan James is a trademark of Morgan James, LLC. www.MorganJamesPublishing.com

Proudly distributed by Publishers Group West®

Morgan James BOGO™

A **FREE** ebook edition is available for you or a friend with the purchase of this print book.

CLEARLY SIGN YOUR NAME ABOVE

Instructions to claim your free ebook edition:
1. Visit MorganJamesBOGO.com
2. Sign your name CLEARLY in the space above
3. Complete the form and submit a photo of this entire page
4. You or your friend can download the ebook to your preferred device

ISBN 9781636981703 paperback
ISBN 9781636981710 ebook
Library of Congress Control Number: 2023933875

Cover & Interior Design by:
Christopher Kirk
www.GFSstudio.com

Morgan James is a proud partner of Habitat for Humanity Peninsula and Greater Williamsburg. Partners in building since 2006.

Get involved today! Visit: www.morgan-james-publishing.com/giving-back

The opportunity to dive deep into the timeless wisdom of two of the greatest coaches of all time, John Wooden and Pat Summitt, has been a treasure and great honor. For both, family was their greatest passion and priority. Fittingly, this book is dedicated to the Wooden and Summitt families through whom the lessons from these legends live on.

CONTENTS

ACKNOWLEDGMENTS:

There are so many remarkable people I want to thank for their vital parts in making this book come to life. First and foremost, I am honored to acknowledge the magnificent teachings and profound wisdom of Coach Wooden and Coach Summitt. Though revered for their basketball success, they always coached people first and basketball second. That is why their impact is eternal. I also want to express my gratitude to Tyler Summitt and to all of Coach Wooden's children and grandchildren for giving these two great coaches their greatest inspiration. To Oprah Winfrey, Michelle Marciniak, LeBron James, Reese Witherspoon, Warren Buffett, Peyton Manning, Michael Phelps, Michelle Obama, Kareem Abdul Jabbar, and Coach Mike Krzyzewski, I am deeply grateful for your stories that demonstrate the real-life application of The Definite Dozen and The Pyramid of Success. I am very appreciative for the terrific contributions I received from Ira and Kim Blumenthal throughout this project. I thank Candace Parker for firing me up with her personal stories about the impact Coach Summitt had on her life. It has been pure joy to work with my editor, Sarah Rexford, as well as the phenomenal team at Morgan James Publishing. Finally, I thank my family for giving me constant, unstoppable purpose and passion in every precious moment.

PREFACE

> "Be more concerned with your character than your
> reputation. For your character is who you are, your
> reputation only what others think you are."
> John Wooden

> "Toughen up, Buttercup!"
> Pat Summitt

S imple human dignity, a focus on character rather than reputation. Humility, never thinking you know it all and always hungry to learn. Generosity and compassion to everyone in need no matter how tough things may be in your own life. Kindness even to those who treat you unfairly. A smile and irrepressible sense of humor even in the face of the cruelest blow one can receive. Purpose centered-not self-centered. Putting the team before yourself. Building loyalty by being loyal. Disagreeing without being disagreeable. Telling the truth even when it's hard to do so. Family first. We-go not ego. Respect for others and yourself. Competitive greatness.

Pat Summitt and John Wooden exemplified all these powerful principles and much, much, more. They were two legendary leaders whose teachings are more important and timely than ever before.

The time has never been more perfect to learn from real heroes: One a man and one a woman. One from the East one from the West. One all passion and intensity, the other calm and even-keeled. Both teaching foundational principles, and most of all, real life examples. They did so to provide a winning game plan to help us all re-focus on character rather than reputation, reason over ratings, humility over hype, and excellence over ego. Not only did Pat Summitt and John Wooden exemplify this extraordinary level of integrity, they proved that it provides a championship formula that generates remarkable results. When you live with this focus, over time, as did these two legends, your character will become your reputation.

Both Coach Wooden and Coach Summitt taught, "It's amazing what's accomplished when no one cares who gets the credit." Credit is something you give while responsibility is something you take. When you demonstrate the correct give and take you build people, teams, and relationships that elevate your family, your community, and the world.

It is so important today for our young people to be exposed to the results that come from honesty, hard work, humility, graciousness, kindness, human compassion, dignity, honor, integrity, and class. Through the examples of these two remarkable people, the lessons and stories in this book shine a light on the astonishing impact that is produced from living with character. Though quite different in style, the essence of their teachings was quite parallel.

Pat Summitt's and John Wooden's timeless teachings come alive in *Lessons from the Legends* through the real-life stories of remarkable present-day leaders from sports and business to entertainment. Leaders like Oprah Winfrey, LeBron James, Reese Witherspoon, Warren Buffett, Peyton Manning, Michael Phelps, Bill and Melinda Gates, Michelle Obama, and Coach Mike Krzyzewski teach us all how wonderful is to focus on what you can GIVE rather than what you can GET!

Lessons from the Legends reminds us that we have a choice every single day to live our lives the way Pat Summitt and John Wooden lived theirs. They made the most of every precious moment. We can do no better than that. I hope their shining examples inspire you to do the same. You'll be better for it.

Brian Biro

Introduction:

MICHELLE MARCINIAK

(At Pat Summitt's funeral, Michelle Marciniak,
one of the great Lady Vols who played for Coach Summitt,
delivered this extraordinary tribute. There is no
better introduction to the teaching, example,
and impact that Pat Summitt brought to the world.)

"There are 161 of us, Pat's former players, and any one of us could be standing up here today. I feel a great deal of humility and responsibility to give you a real sense of who Pat was to us.

We are all hurting. The sadness we are feeling is unexplainable because it seems so unfair. I ask myself why? Why Pat, Lord? Why did you pick her to fight this awful disease? And why did you take one of the finest women to ever set foot on this earth in a short five years?

We looked up to her. She was our coach and our role model, our mentor and our friend. She was a superhero. I can't help but ask these questions.

Honestly, I'm angry. That's how I feel. This disease is awful. Pat would still be coaching on the sidelines today if it weren't for Alzheimer's. I want to find a cure because it killed my coach. It killed her. That's reality.

But I guess that's just it. We are not in control of our final destiny. And we know from Pat's passing that we are never promised tomorrow.

This is where faith comes in and Pat had a ton of it. I have to admit that my road with Pat was not a smooth one but because she had faith, and so did I. I knew that her heart was always in the right place. And for that reason alone, I respected and trusted her.

All of us former players are the lucky ones. We've been given a blessing to have been coached by Pat, to learn from her, to watch her, to go into battle with her, and to experience her presence in person through the good times and bad.

We ask ourselves, what are we to learn from this?

You know, we watched film endlessly with Pat. She wanted us to analyze, listen, and learn. She would monitor and then wanted us to self-monitor. She would teach us and coach us in those film sessions and wanted us to own our mistakes so that we wouldn't make the same mistakes again.

Because of that, we owned our successes and failures. She knew something we didn't and she guided us toward what she knew, but she always made us finish the last lap.

I believe with my whole heart that Pat would want us to be strong for her during these difficult days that led into and will depart from her death. I know for me personally she hated when I started to cry. She used to always say, "Quit your cryin' Marciniak." And she said many times after being diagnosed, "Don't throw a pity party for me." She meant it. There was no room for excuses, not even good ones.

When I first arrived on campus, seeing how visible the Lady Vol program was and how public Pat expected us to be, I felt the need to share with Pat that I grew up with a speech impediment. I stuttered. Therefore, I had a great fear of speaking and told her that I would not be comfortable speaking in public and introducing myself. Pat looked at me with her steely stare and responded simple, concise, and direct. Shetold me to get over it.

I was stunned and offended at her lack of empathy, but I learned later that she saw it as an opportunity for me to grow. She tested me time and time again because from that point on when we would be in any setting, and Pat was always the grand marshal of every event or dinner, she would say, "Do any of our players have anything to say. Michelle?"

She put me on the spot. She made me speak. She made me face my fears. My biggest accomplishment playing for Pat was not winning a national championship, it was speaking.

Speaking at the Sears trophy presentation and on ESPN immediately following our Championship game. Speaking at the White House. Speaking as an entrepreneur and then speaking for Pat whenever I could when she was diagnosed with Alzheimer's.

The confidence she instilled within me to stand up and speak out was life changing. Pat helped me discover a voice I didn't know I had. If she did this for me, imagine what she did for the 160 other players.

From the compassion she had for Chamique (Holdsclaw) to walk her through her illness, to the endless support Pat gave me in being an entrepreneur, this was Pat at her core. Pat was all about her players and finding out ways to help us become better people and better professionals, post-career.

Pat had a way at finding just the perfect time to enter and re-enter our lives and offer love and support.

I think Kara (Lawson) said it best when she said that Pat lives in each of us every day.

As I thought about what I wanted to say today, I thought about you, Hazel, a mother who just lost her daughter. I thought about you, Tommy and Charles and Kenneth and Linda, siblings who just lost their sister. I thought about you, Tyler, a son who just lost his mother.

As most people know, Tyler was nearly born in my living room during Pat's recruiting visit, so we have always shared a special bond.

Tyler, as you might remember, we were at the *Sports Illustrated* Sportsman of the Year awards in 2011 just after Pat's diagnosis. You and Pat were sitting in the front row that night. I had written a tribute for her that I delivered at the ceremony. As I thought about what to say today, I went back to that tribute because to me, it captured the essence of who Pat was at her core. So here we go:

"Who Is This Woman"

A bond of everlasting proportion in 1990

A truly unique moment that you and I shared together

His name is Tyler

The amazing blessing you brought into this world

Your son kicking inside of you as you sat in my living room

Toughing it out, as you do with every aspect of your life

I thought, "Who is this woman?"

In my home, 9 months pregnant

Fighting nature to sacrifice for…for what?

The answer came clear to me as I learned about who you are at your core.

Your sacrifice to sign a recruit in your condition went beyond the norm. It was about them, not you. Them being the people you were sacrificing for at the University of Tennessee who believed in you, who gave you the opportunity of your lifetime

Fighting for those who trusted in you to do anything and everything you could to not only win championships but most importantly to influence lives—young and old—family, players, fans, friends, administration, colleagues, former coaches and teammates.

The legacy you built from the ground up was coming into play in my own living room as you chose to grind through the pains of labor and make a trip against the doctor's better judgment.

I was beginning to embark upon a journey in which I would come under the incredible influence of a classy, strong-willed woman in my life.

I soon learned this when I stepped foot on campus, in
your office, on your court, into your world.

"Who is this woman?" continually crossed my mind
after spending more time with you.

This woman is a fighter.

She's a competitor.

She doesn't accept mediocrity.

She's never satisfied.

I've never met anyone like her.

In her eyes, there was always more.

More perfection.

I didn't think I could ever get it right.

You made every day the greatest challenge of my life.

You made me start over each day.

Perfecting yesterday.

Never looking for tomorrow.

Taking care of today.

Repeating patterns of near perfection.

Just when I thought I was close to receiving your
compliment.

You said do it again.

This time do it better.

"Who is this woman?" I thought over and over again.

So surprising to me was what came next.

In so many frustrating tears and sanity checks.

As I was experiencing growing pains like never before.

Searching for my own connection to perfection.

Trying to please you and feeling as if I was failing mis-
erably at every turn.

What I received time and time again when I was at my
absolute breaking point.

Was not a compliment from you.

Rather, you hugged my neck.

You cared.

You spent endless hours with me, teaching me.

You showed me you loved me through the time you
spent with me.

You said to me, "You'll understand why I am doing this
one day."

There's a bigger picture.

Hang in there.

I am pushing you because you can take it.

Because I believe in you.

Because I know you have what it takes.

You said, "Trust me.

I will not allow you to fail under my watch."

You said, "I need for you to be tougher."

In my weaker moments, I asked you to ease up on me.

You said, "Stop your crying."

I cried harder.

I said, "I don't think I can do this anymore."

You said, "Yes you can, we're getting there."

You said, "Trust me. There's a reason for this."

In my own kicking and fighting in trying to understand
what you were attempting to get out of me I was
always listening. You had my attention.

You kept saying it will be worth it. I need for you to get
through this with me.

"Who is this woman?" How did she command such a presence in my soul from the very moment we met, a presence that only intensified over the following months and years?

All the while, teaching me the greatest lessons of my life:

It wasn't about me.

It was about my teammates.

It was about the Tennessee program.

It was about others.

It was about showing up and bringing your best every single day.

Learning more.

Here comes the full circle.

You come into the Tennessee program as a superstar

And you leave as a Champion, not just on the basketball court but in life.

What a powerful revelation and feeling to understand the tremendous difference between the two.

You didn't just make us better. You made us the best at who we were trying to become.

You were not only being tough. You were teaching toughness.

You never did anything for your own glory. You worked your magic through selfless acts of kindness.

You didn't raise your voice just for the sake of it. You increased your tone to demand excellence.

You didn't rush any process. You taught patience and urgency through a painstaking refining regimen.

Not only were you a perfectionist, you were a master at sculpting your masterpiece.

For a woman who has accomplished what you have in basketball, you had every right to display arrogance. Instead, you displayed the most precious humility.

Together, we won. And won it all. Accomplishments we've all celebrated through all the days of our lives.

What I learned, though, is the one thing I carry with me as I remember you telling me that "I will understand one day."

Here it is: Life is not about accomplishments, wins or losses. It's about investing in people and relationships. The greatest reward in life is a result of sacrificing yourself for another human being in order to help them become their best.

I now see the bigger picture

Pat, you've sacrificed for us all and now it's our turn to pay it forward.

You fought the battle that allowed the game of basketball to be what it is today.

You fought the battle to create opportunities for us and you taught us how to win.

And you courageously fought the battle of Alzheimer's and publicly put a face to this dreadful disease so that the world will join us in the fight to find a cure.

Pat, we are so much better because of you. We do see who you were and from this day forward we will band together and tuck you in and carry you with us in our souls, forever.

Michelle Marciniak
July 9th, 2016

1.

SCALE THE SUMMIT WITH THE DEFINITE DOZEN: RESPECT YOURSELF AND OTHERS

One of the great challenges in coaching major college basketball at the highest level is that every player you recruit arrives at your university having been THE star on their high school team. They have always been the "big fish." Now they are surrounded by athletes with similar talent and pedigree. How does a coach transform ego into "we go?" How do you move from silos to synergy?

Coach Summitt knew that the essential ingredient required to transform talent into team and "me" into "we" was respect.

Even when some of her players had strikingly different personalities and styles, even when they simply did not mesh with each other off the court, she knew that great things could happen if they could build authentic and mutual respect for one another. But most importantly, Coach Summitt also knew that there could be no real respect for one another until they respected themselves.

There is an immense difference between self-respect and arrogance or conceit. Coach believed you can only earn your own self-respect through living your word and as what she often called, "walking your talk." She believed it is about character, not reputation. As one of Pat Summitt's heroes, Coach John Wooden said, "Your character is who you are. Your reputation only what others think you are."

You build self-respect by doing what you believe to be right whether or not anyone is watching. This self-respect comes from constantly focusing on what you put in to each day, your effort, energy, and attitude.

Only when you have earned your own self-respect will you be able to look others in the eye, become a great team member, and treat others with dignity and respect. Then, you will honor and appreciate others for their gifts and contributions without feeling threatened.

Pat Summitt knew that only with self-respect and respecting others are great things possible. Growing up on a Tennessee farm, her father demanded respect and her mother demonstrated it every single day through her remarkable work ethic and the way she treated others. They each taught her that there is an enormous difference between knowing what to do and doing what you know, and that respect can only be earned by doing the latter. You will never breakthrough until you follow through and live according to your highest principles and commitments.

When she went off to college, she felt shy about her long, gangly appearance and her folksy way of talking. However, the powerful inner core of self-respect and resolve that her family had built within her enabled her to know she could overcome any obstacle and face any challenge with confidence.

Immense self-respect was shown at the 2018 ESPY awards as more than 140 women gathered on stage to accept the Arthur Ashe Award for Courage, the same award Pat Summitt received in 2012. These women, representing many different sports, were the survivors from more than 30 years of reprehensible sexual abuse by Dr. Larry Nasser. He had used his position as the physician responsible for the physical well-being of these young women as the perfect vehicle to systematically and diabolically take advantage of them. At each treatment session he went just a little further and disguised the abuse under the false umbrella of treatment.

In many ways just as insidious, these young women were the survivors of coverups from many who could have helped. They were the victims of not being heard and of being gagged and shamed whenever they tried to speak up. They had been teenagers when the abuse and the pressure to hide the truth and keep their stories to themselves began. Every single day that they lived in silence about the abuse, holding in the embarrassment and the self-doubt that filled them, a desperate battle raged in their spirit.

Should they go on being dominated and controlled by the regimented obedience that had been drilled into them throughout their athletic training? Should they continue listening to those who told them to keep quiet and follow their guidance without question? Or should they acknowledge the painful truth that something was horribly wrong in the way they had been treated? Should they acknowledge that their self-respect was being beaten down and their voices being silenced by those who would not listen? Every day these teenaged athletes received the powerful subliminal message from authority figures they had been trained to trust that their honor, well-being, and self-respect were not as important as medals, money, and reputations.

But on this night, in front of the finest athletes and coaches in the world and a global television audience of millions, these brave young women stood tall. They proclaimed to all that their self-respect would never again bow down to abuse and to those who would seek to quiet their voices. They refused to give up and be controlled or silenced any longer.

By demonstrating their self-respect that night, those 140 incredible young women undoubtedly prevented thousands and thousands of others from experiencing the pain they had been forced to endure. The respect they exemplified as they stood strong together gave powerful notice to predators that their game was up.

Even more important, these women, who now call themselves the Sister Survivors, taught millions of others that night—young women and men of all races, nationalities, and faiths—to never, ever allow anyone to threaten, steal, or abuse their self-respect.

The spirit of Pat Summitt was there with them that night, watching, smiling and filled with pride in this sisterhood. They clearly understood the messages she powerfully imparted to every Lady Vol: "Toughen up, buttercup. Be who you are. You earn and build respect inch by inch. Left foot, right foot, breathe. You are important."

2.

TAKE FULL RESPONSIBILITY

It's amazing what can be accomplished when no one cares who gets the credit. Credit is something you GIVE, responsibility something you TAKE! There's an old adage, "If it's to be it's up to me. If things are to change, I must change!" Coach Pat Summitt believed that the greatest birthright we are given is personal responsibility. We are given around 800,000 hours or so. What we do with those hours is called our life. And what we do with our life ultimately depends upon the responsibility we take for our choices and actions.

Coach also believed that the only way she could effectively teach others to take responsibility was to exemplify it. She was a supreme "blame-buster" for she understood that blame serves no constructive, long-term purpose. When you consider blame in the context of time, is blame about the past, present, or future? Clearly, blame is always about the past. Can you do anything about the past? Of course, you can't! So, whenever you get caught up in blame you put yourself in the past where there can be no progress, change, and improvement.

As a dedicated blame-buster, Coach Summitt did not pretend that mistakes weren't made. On the contrary, she was very clear, straight-forward, honest, and often intense about what had been done incorrectly, inappropriately, or even thoughtlessly. But then, she very deliberately moved the focus to the present by centering on what was best to do next and what must be learned from that misstep. She constantly stressed responsibility over blame.

When leaders blame others, their teams are afraid to act, to take risks, innovate, and disrupt the status quo. When, on the other hand, leaders teach and exemplify personal responsibility, they ignite an atmosphere of energy, creativity, and confidence.

It has often been said that one of the most essential ingredients in creating success is failure. It is not how many times you fall that matters, but rather how often you rise up again. Only when you fully accept personal responsibility does failure serve you. It is the secret to resilience. Only when you embrace personal responsibility does failure transform into learning and breakthroughs. Only then can you move forward because you understand that where you are is not who you are!

J.K. Rowling is perhaps the most famous author on planet earth. Her *Harry Potter* series has sold more than 400 million copies and inspired a generation to read, to imagine, and to dream. But those remarkable stories would never have been written, would never have touched so many lives, had she not accepted personal responsibility for a life that was filled with obstacles, poverty, and setbacks. Had she blamed her parents for not creating a home filled with love, joy, and energy when she was growing up, or had she given up on herself and her dreams when she was penniless, divorced, jobless, and a single mom with a young daughter who needed her, our world would have far less magic in it today. But she took responsibility to do what she felt she was here to do, to write the incredible story of a boy with a lightning scar who would never give up.

Every single one of the twelve major publishers who read her manuscript in 1995 rejected the series. Finally, a year later, a small, independent publisher, Bloomsbury, said yes and printed the first of the *Harry Potter* books. Her advance was a pittance of 1,500 pounds. Four hundred million copies later (and still growing) her royalties from book sales and the various *Harry Potter* enterprises from theme parks to blockbuster movies made J.K. Rowling a billionaire and one of the three wealthiest women in the world.

Just like Pat Summitt, throughout her life, J.K. Rowling has never stopped taking personal responsibility for doing what she believes to be right. At the peak of her fortune, she made the decision to give away a huge portion of her wealth to causes that inspired her, including charities focused on alleviating poverty and hunger, on elevating literacy, on finding a cure for multiple sclerosis from which her mother died, and on improving conditions for children throughout Europe. That decision, though sharply lowering her position on the list of wealthiest women on earth, made her far richer in ways that truly matter. As she said so powerfully, "I think you have a moral responsibility when you've been given far more than you need to do wise things with it and give intelligently." That is precisely the same spirit and commitment that Pat Summitt demonstrated to the world when she announced that she had been diagnosed with early onset Alzheimer's and founded the Pat Summitt Foundation. This foundation's mission is to help others stricken with the insidious disease and to eventually find a cure.

LeBron James, who deeply admired Pat Summitt, is one of the most recognizable, successful, and admired athletes on earth. He is widely considered the greatest basketball player of his generation. But as extraordinary as his talent, work ethic, and accomplishments are, his greatest and most vital strength is his determination to accept responsibility for his decisions and actions. It is this responsibility that will continue to make his greatest impact long after his basketball days are done.

Like so many of those around him, growing up in the poorest sections of Akron, Ohio, every single day young LeBron found himself in the midst of poverty, drugs, and violence. He knew all too well what it was to live with hunger and homelessness. As he often said as he looked back, "I'm just a kid from Akron. I'm not supposed to be here. I'm supposed to be a statistic."

In the fourth grade he missed over 80 days of school. It was at that pivotal moment in his life that a couple of coaches and teachers took responsibility to give LeBron some structure, guidance, and care. For the first time in his life they gave him a vision that he could become more than his circumstances. They believed in LeBron more than he had ever believed in himself and demanded of him what Pat Summitt demanded of every Lady Vol—that he raise his expectations of himself athletically, academically, and as a human being. In the fifth grade LeBron didn't miss a day of school and he started an ascension as a student, basketball player, and leader that keeps rising ever higher.

Throughout his phenomenal career, LeBron has never stopped accepting responsibility to make a difference for kids just like him. He continues to speak out for what he believes, even when chided to "Shut up and dribble." When you fully accept responsibility, you refuse to let naysayers and critics silence you or inhibit your passion. LeBron has an unstoppable vision to help these disadvantaged children from the streets of Akron become very different kinds of statistics. His vision is to help them become the kind of statistics that meant the most to Pat Summitt and John Wooden: College graduates, doctors, teachers, community leaders, and responsible, inspired parents who teach their children that anything is possible. He believes that as a direct result of changing the statistics of what those young people become, literacy rates will rise dramatically, drug use will diminish, crime rates and homelessness will drop, and countless lives will be improved.

In July of 2018 the LeBron James Family Foundation opened what he considers his greatest accomplishment—more than his career scoring record, more than his Championships, more than his MVP awards—the I Promise School in his hometown of Akron. This school represented a new model for helping disadvantaged children learn personal responsibility, structure, boundaries, and character. At the I Promise School the academic day is longer. School stays in session until 5 PM so the students have more time learning and less time on the streets. Meals and snacks are provided because LeBron understands from his own experience that hungry children have a much harder time focusing and engaging.

Everywhere the children and faculty look at the I Promise School, they see inspirational quotes, photos, and images of possibility, positive attitude, gratitude, and vision. Three hundred third and fourth graders walked through the doors of the I Promise School that first day and met a giant of a man with tears of joy in his eyes and a smile that shined with hope for each and every one of them. Accepting and exercising personal responsibility is the only way to change the world for the better.

Like J.K. Rowling and LeBron James, Pat Summitt was not afraid to make mistakes, nor was she disappointed in her players when they made them, so long as their effort and intensity was strong. But, she was fiercely determined not to repeat them. She expressed her philosophy of personal responsibility this way: "Accountability is essential to personal growth, as well as team growth. How can you improve if you're never wrong? If you don't admit a mistake and take responsibility for it, you're bound to make the same one again."

Another legendary coach, Paul "Bear" Bryant of Alabama football expressed the essence of this vital principle of taking full responsibility when he said in his simple, no-nonsense way: "I'm just an old country plow-hand, but I've learned one thing. If you want to build a team whose heart beats as one, when things go great, THEY did it. When things go pretty good, WE did it. When things go bad, I did it." What a powerful way to instill loyalty and inspire peak performance among your team members, just as Pat Summitt did, by teaching responsibility through example!

3.

DEMONSTRATE AND DEVELOP LOYALTY

B y far the greatest influence and source of purpose in Pat Summitt's life, just as it was for John Wooden, was family. As much as she loved basketball, competition, and winning, family always came first. So, it is not surprising that she created and nurtured the family model within Tennessee basketball. Her assistant coaches stayed with her for decades through both triumphs and travails and every up and every down because she treated them as so much more than paid employees. To Pat Summitt, they were family. And to her, loyalty to family was absolute.

When Coach Summitt talked about loyalty it is powerfully revealing to notice that the conversation always started with her focus on being loyal, not on receiving loyalty. Pat did not want a team of coaches who were just like her. Her humility allowed her to see that if she surrounded herself with yes people, people who simply pandered to her every decision, Tennessee basketball would not go very far.

She wanted coaches who she believed were better than her in areas that she knew were not her greatest strengths. She wanted coaches who would challenge her and call her out when they felt her actions or emotions were becoming counter-productive. When she found those coaches, Holly Warlick, Mickie Demoss, Nancy Darsch, Al Brown, and others, she became intensely loyal to them. She saw them as family. She created an environment where her coaches were free to tell her what she needed to hear, not just what she wanted to hear. She gave them both responsibility and authority and created loyalty in the only enduring way, by treating them with trust, gratitude, and ultimate respect.

When your focus is first and foremost on giving loyalty, receiving it in return is simply the natural result. You can't demand loyalty, but you can choose to be loyal and then support that decision by being 100% consistent in the way you speak about others. Loyalty is the "we go" versus "ego" principle.

When Mickie and Nancy moved on from Tennessee, pursuing other career opportunities after many years as assistant coaches, Pat did not waiver in the glowing, positive, and deeply appreciative way she spoke about them. She stayed in constant contact when they left. She wasn't loyal when they were there and disloyal when they weren't. This consistency and constant loyalty spoke volumes to everyone around Pat Summitt. They knew that her loyalty was not conditional, nor was it temporary.

It was unconditional and permanent. When Pat Summitt was loyal to you it was for life. The confidence and inspiration that results from such loyalty cannot be measured.

Coach Summitt believed passionately that human beings will do more for others than they'll do for themselves. It was perhaps the most important truth to her about the human spirit and the power of a team. Loyalty provides the turbo fuel for unstoppable inspiration. Only when you are unshakingly loyal to your teammates will you be able to perform at your ultimate level.

Pat Summitt's great friend and Tennessee grad, Peyton Manning, played quarterback for the Indianapolis Colts from 1999 to 2011. He was as admired and respected for his tireless work in his community as he was for his incomparable work ethic and legendary football genius. He poured so much love, time, and energy into the children's section of St. Vincent Hospital in Indy, that in 2007 it was renamed the Peyton Manning Children's Hospital.

In 2012, after enduring a brutal neck injury that many experts thought would have ended his career, Manning moved on to quarterback the Denver Broncos. But in typical Peyton fashion, he dove into his rehab the way he devoured game tapes, with a passion and determination that was unstoppable. He came back from that surgery to have perhaps the finest year ever delivered by an NFL quarterback. He led the Broncos to the Super Bowl and broke records for yardage and touchdown passes in a season. A couple of seasons later, he led the Broncos to his second Super Bowl Championship.

One might think that with the enormous focus required to accomplish his astonishing recovery and then deliver such an unprecedented performance for his new team, Peyton's loyalty to the children's hospital would surely wane. There are just so many hours in a day. But Manning, very much like his friend and mentor Pat Summitt, highly values loyalty.

Throughout his rehab from surgery, continuing nonstop during his playing days with Denver, and now years after his retirement as one of the greatest players of all-time, Peyton Manning has never stopped pouring his heart and soul into helping those children. He has called hundreds and hundreds of them (always asking the parents first if it is okay for him to speak with their children directly). And when he calls these children, many of whom are fighting for their young lives, above all, he listens. He is fully present for each and every child he speaks with and that pure presence communicates to them that he deeply cares. Peyton is passing on to these children and their families a foundational principle he heard many times from Coach Summitt: "People don't care how much you know, until they know how much you care."

Peyton makes the children feel that they are the heroes and that he is genuinely in awe of their spirit. Just like Pat Summitt, he has never sought to publicize his remarkable loyalty. On the contrary, he has tried to keep this story private because he doesn't connect with these children to receive publicity or praise. He does it because he sees these children as extended family who need to know that they are loved and supported. He does it out of loyalty to his highest values and beliefs. The inner happiness he receives when he knows a child's day has become a little bit brighter because he cared enough to call is what inspires Peyton to keep making those calls.

The joy that comes from giving without worrying about what you'll receive in return is the unsolicited bonus that you will receive when you demonstrate genuine loyalty. For only when you give it away will it come back to you, just as Pat Summitt lived and taught every day of her life.

4.

LEARN TO BE A GREAT COMMUNICATOR

Many would be surprised to learn that early in their careers Pat Summitt and John Wooden, two of the greatest coaches and communicators ever, were both very shy and terribly frightened of speaking in public. Our lasting vision of each of them was of highly confident, clear, and tremendously wise speakers and teachers. However, this transformation took great focus and work. Both had to learn to breakthrough their fears and lack of confidence.

These two legendary coaches understood how vital it was to become a great communicator. Both of them humbly approached what they knew to be a real weakness with unstoppable determination to learn and improve.

The question arises, "What does it mean to be a great communicator?" For Coach Summitt, a foundational principle was at the heart of true communication excellence: The meaning of my communication is the response I generate.

Put simply, it didn't matter if Coach Summitt thought she had been extremely clear, articulate, and inspiring. What mattered to her was far more practical and fundamental. Had her communication worked? Had it generated her desired outcome? Had it led to understanding and results? Was she sure she truly had communicated what she intended?

The automatic outcomes of committing to this definition of great communication are personal responsibility and flexibility. If the meaning of my communication is the response I generate, then if someone does not connect with what I'm saying, I will take personal responsibility to change myself. It's not that they're not bright enough. It's not that they didn't pay enough attention. It's simply that my communication did not work. And when it's not working, try something different! Coach Summitt was alert, agile, and adaptable in her communication because she realized that everyone is different in the way they hear, learn, and develop. She understood that if the effectiveness of her communication was to change and improve, she had to change and improve. Just as it did for Pat Summitt and John Wooden, learning to be a great communicator can dramatically change your life.

For his first 28 years, Bill Walton, one of the greatest basketball players of all time, literally could not string a full sentence together without stuttering horribly. A three-time NCAA college basketball player of the year during his time at UCLA playing for John Wooden, MVP of the NBA, and world champion with the Portland Trail Blazers, Walton's refuge, his religion, was basketball. It was his safe haven, his Eden where he could escape the embarrassment of his speech impediment and overpower it with his physical and mental gifts on the hardwood. But after more than 30 operations on his congenitally damaged feet, on knees that had been worn to dust, and on his back that had been broken in two places at twenty-one, his basketball days seemed over. He was lost and floundering, trying to find a new direction for his professional life that would fill the gaping hole the game he loved had filled.

Though unable to function on the court, Walton still sought to find a way to stay connected to the game and to develop a new direction for his career where he could utilize his passion and expertise. Always a free-spirit and possibility thinker, this fun-loving, six foot eleven inches, nearly crippled stutterer naturally decided upon the most outrageous course of action: Becoming a sportscaster!

Drawing upon the lessons about hard work, focus, preparation, and intent that he learned from Coach Wooden (and that so perfectly parallel the teaching of Pat Summitt through the Definite Dozen), Walton dove into this new challenge. He worked to overcome a life-time of stuttering with determination, enthusiasm, and a clear plan. From Hall of Fame sportscaster Marty Glickman, Walton gathered some simple, clear tips he worked on every single day in pursuit of his vision to become a successful broadcaster.

Glickman taught him to slow his thoughts down and to think only about what he was saying in the present moment instead of several sentences ahead. He encouraged Walton to read out loud whenever he could and to do so in front of a mirror to simulate being watched while on television. He taught Walton to chew sugar free gum constantly to strengthen his speaking muscles and to get his mouth moving. He worked overtime on the particular sounds that gave him the greatest trouble, repeating them over and over until he could handle them smoothly. Most importantly, Glickman encouraged Walton to look at his stumbles and setbacks as perhaps his greatest teachers, to stop, reset, and get back on track.

Due to rehabbing his endless injuries, Walton understood that becoming a great communicator is a marathon, not a sprint. Walton knew that marathons are run inch by inch, step by step, and mile by mile. But when you know your destination, and you've trained for that twenty-six-mile race by running 26,000 miles in practice, you can breakthrough even twenty-eight years of an extreme speech impediment.

Walton, the man who could not so much as say thank you without stumbling, became a Hall of Fame broadcaster himself and fittingly, a key spokesperson for the Stuttering Foundation. As Bill Walton, John Wooden, and Pat Summitt would tell you, if they could become great communicators, so can you! The impact that skill will have on everyone you touch will be immeasurable.

5.

DISCIPLINE YOURSELF SO NO ONE ELSE HAS TO

Like all great coaches and leaders, Pat Summitt did not believe you should treat everyone exactly the same. Some of her players needed to be pushed and challenged. Some thrived on more praise. Others just needed an occasional pat on the back or to simply give them the ball and get out of the way. Still others required a very pointed pat with her toe targeted at their backside. Pat's passion and genius was in learning all she could about each of her players, what inspired them, what built them, and what brought out the best in them.

When it came to discipline, Coach Summitt was steadfast. Discipline must be the same for everyone. She was an equal opportunity disciplinarian. Discipline must be consistent, firm, and fair.

There is no faster way to destroy synergy and respect on a team than to administer discipline unequally. There can be no playing favorites. The rules must be fair and aimed at solving problems or potential problems before they materialize. The consequences for breaking those rules must be clear, consistent, and firm.

Disciplinary measures should not be compromised. Coach Summitt wanted her players to know the rules and the consequences up front so they knew what was coming if they tried to sneak around a rule or consciously break one. She also wanted her players to believe that if they did try to hide an infraction, if they broke curfew or missed class, Pat would know.

She loved fostering the myth (though it wasn't all that far from the truth!) that she was ever-present and omniscient, because although she was known as a strict disciplinarian, her hope was to never have to discipline! Instead, by being firm, fair, and consistent, she wanted to instill self-discipline. She knew this was the most enduring, effective, and positive form of discipline, and she demanded nothing less from herself.

When you are self-disciplined you hold yourself to high standards. Self-discipline is respect-based while punishment is fear-based. When discipline is administered fairly, firmly, and consistently, you bring structure and clarity to the team environment. You kill the monster before it grows. You make it blatantly clear that actions have consequences and that though you have a choice about your actions, the consequences are automatic. Self-discipline is enduring and habitual and removes the need for external discipline. By exercising self-discipline, you exemplify genuine integrity: Doing the right thing when no one else is watching.

The story of Michael Phelps' swimming achievements is the stuff of legend. His story (twenty-eight Olympic medals and twenty-three of them gold) powerfully demonstrates this vitally important Pat Summitt Definite Dozen principle. In the 2008 Games in Beijing, Phelps won an astonishing eight Gold Medals. He earned one by a hundredth of a second, when he almost miraculously overcame a half-body length deficit in the final few meters. He was the ultimate competitor, a force of nature, a super-hero who fired-up the dreams of millions of young swimmers around the globe.

As incredible as his story of athletic triumph is, there is a more powerful and important story about Michael Phelps. It is a story of transformation, of moving from fear to freedom, and from failure to faith because Michael Phelps made the decision to discipline himself before others had to.

Michael emerged from his history-making performance in Beijing and seemed to be on top of the world. His dominant performance was the greatest Olympic achievement of all-time in any sport. Companies were lining up to sign this All-American hero to six and seven-figure endorsement contracts. He made swimming glamorous and exciting as he inspired a new generation to take up the sport.

But inside, Michael was lost. He had spent virtually every moment of his young life devoted to the single-minded obsession to climb his Everest. But now that he had reached the summit, he was seized with emptiness, self-doubt, and the paralyzing fear that he now had nowhere else to go.

To most of the outside world it didn't make any sense. He seemed to have it all—wealth, fame, and the adoration of millions of fans worldwide. But Michael had no idea who he was outside of the pool. After years of laser-like focus and discipline he had lost his motivation and energy.

He started partying and drinking and missed more and more workouts. When he was photographed at a party with a bong, the image went viral. Rather than waking him up, the embarrassment and humiliation that was stirred up by the photo caused Michael to become increasingly guarded and wary of people. He started hanging out more and more with those who encouraged his partying and defiance and pushed his most important relationships away. He argued constantly with his long-time coach, Bob Bowman, and keeping anyone who truly cared about him at arms-length. Not even his mother and sister, who had been there for Michael every moment of his life, could reach him. He was terrified about what he would do for the rest of his life. Swimming became a temporary escape instead of a passion.

At the 2012 Olympics in London, Michael somehow managed to win another six medals including four golds. But he knew those medals were tarnished. He had won them through sheer talent and knew in his heart he had skated through training. He had not given his all. He left those games more lost than ever, fell deeper into feelings of worthlessness and depression, and desperately afraid to reveal his vulnerability, hid behind an image he knew was a lie.

In 2014 he was arrested for the second time for a DUI after drinking heavily at a Baltimore casino. For three days after he was released on bail, Michael Phelps, the all-time Olympic Champion, locked himself in his house and refused to speak with anyone. He thought seriously about taking his own life. He reached rock bottom.

But in the darkest moments of his life, Michael did one crucial thing that most in his position never do. He never blamed anyone else for his mistakes, never made excuses for where he found himself. He took personal responsibility for what he had done, and deep down, he accepted that if things were to change, he must change. He decided to discipline himself and make the choice to alter his direction before others had to. He faced up to his fear and his emptiness and decided to get better rather than bitter.

He had himself admitted as an inpatient at the Meadows, an alcohol, drug, and depression rehab clinic in Arizona. Over the next six weeks he opened himself up as he had never done before. He expressed his vulnerability and fears. He began to read books about purpose, peace of mind, and personal leadership. The others at the clinic saw him as a human being, not as Michael Phelps the Olympic Champion, the machine, or the superhero. Each day he began to see himself in this same new way and to discover who he really was.

For the first time he found that he could let go of what everybody else thought about him and accept and enjoy who he was as a person. No one can be loved until they let themselves be seen. No one can be seen until they learn to love themselves. As he forgave himself, he learned to forgive others. He reached out to his estranged father of many years and they began to heal wounds he had previously thought were permanent. He emerged from rehab excited about being himself, about becoming a father, husband, and servant leader who wanted to help others as so many had tried to help him.

Michael dove back into swimming with a new kind of passion. No longer was he trying to show the world that he was a champion or competing merely to add to his record medal count. He swam now to fulfill himself and to be able to leave the sport on his terms with no regrets. He trained harder for the Rio games than he ever had before. But now he swam because he loved the sport. He swam to feel the joy of knowing he was giving his best, rather than because he felt he had to perform for everyone else.

Michael's adoring family came to watch: His mother, his sister, his fiancée who would soon become his wife, his baby boy, Boomer (who wore special headphones during Michael's races so the deafening cheering wouldn't harm his little ears), and his father he had invited back into his life. In front of them all, Michael walked off the Olympic pool deck in Rio for the last time with six more medals, five of them gold.

He was chosen as captain by his teammates and selected as the flag bearer for the United States for the Opening Ceremonies. When he won the silver medal in the one-hundred-meter butterfly, he was more than gracious in defeat. He was genuinely proud of the young man who had beaten him, Joseph Schooling of Singapore, who had trained with Michael in the United States. Virtually every teammate on the U.S. Olympic Swimming team praised Phelps for his leadership, team spirit, and desire to serve.

Michael Phelps' decision to discipline himself before others had to, to accept responsibility for his actions and choices, and to hold himself to a higher standard as a human being has made him a far greater champion than ever before. This is the lesson

Pat Summitt taught every Lady Vol every day of her career. When you do the same, when you are determined to discipline yourself before others have to, you will live with real integrity. You will discover the peace of mind that only comes when you do the right thing when no one is watching.

6.

MAKE HARD WORK
YOUR PASSION

Do you absolutely love what you do? Does the thought of your work energize you and fire up your spirit? Do you approach your day-to-day responsibilities and duties with a "like to, love to, can't wait to" spirit or more of a "have to" attitude? Does the thought of hard work and challenge inspire you or expire you?

Sadly, for many, hard work is only seen as hard! It is only through attention to small details, repetition, and focused effort that mastery is built. So, until you learn to love the work, it is highly unlikely you will ever approach your real potential.

It is so easy to look at superstars from the world of sports and believe that their astonishing careers were simply due to DNA and unmatched natural ability. Consider athletes such as Michael Jordan, LeBron James, Michael Phelps, Katie Ledecky, Simone Biles, Peyton Manning, Tom Brady, Roger Federer, Serena Williams, and others. All of these remarkable athletes have certainly been blessed with great talent. But it was because they made hard work their passion that they created such remarkable results.

As talented as they all are, none are overachievers, and neither are you! All of them have striven daily to improve and to approach their potential. This was only possible because their passion was in the journey and the work more than in the destination. Without that passion, they never would have had the resilience to keep challenging themselves. There are many factors outside of their control that affect whether they win or lose. They know they do not actually control the results of their hard work. They do control their preparation, effort, energy, and focus. The same is true for you.

Coach Summitt loved the daily practices even more than the games. Practices provided her and her assistants with the opportunity to do what they loved most—to teach. This was where they felt they could make the biggest difference and generate the greatest impact. When you love hard work, you are constantly in motion and on purpose. To be filled with purpose is to live a rich and fulfilling life!

Richard Head, Pat Summitt's father, was tough, intimidating, and unyielding. He believed that working hard was God-ordained and gave our lives definition, direction, and purpose. He believed it brought out the best in us. Though he found it nearly impossible to show affection in any way, he was quick to demonstrate his feelings of dissatisfaction through powerful application of the belt. Pat grew up with an insatiable yearning to win her father's love and respect. His influence on the kind of coach, leader, and human being that she became was enormous. Most of the lessons he taught were the result of very tough love.

Hazel Head, Pat's mother, on the other hand, was mild-spoken, patient, kind, generous, and loving. She left the disciplining of her children to Richard. But, oh my how she worked! Like her daughter's championship teams, Hazel was in constant and focused motion. She never stopped. Her way of teaching was through an unselfish, never-complaining example.

Though their styles were almost completely opposite, in no area did Richard and Hazel have more impact on Pat than in teaching her to make hard work a passion. There is a very important distinction between simply working hard and making hard work your passion. When you become a hard worker because you believe that is what you are supposed to do, you do so from a "have to" perspective.

Whenever you do anything because you think you have to, two other words come into play: Or else. In other words, you have to work hard or else something bad will happen. "Have to" choices are fear-based. But when you make hard work a passion, you do so from a "like to, want to, can't wait to, love to" perspective. When hard work is your passion, it is love-based, not fear based.

What do Mary Barra (the first female CEO of General Motors), LeBron James, Mark Cuban (tech magnate, TV personality, and owner of the Dallas Mavericks), and Apple CEO Tim Cook all have in common? Most definitely, it's not their jump shots! It's not even their net worth, though there is a powerfully similar pattern when it comes to their financial status. No, there's one magical ingredient they all share that has set them apart as icons in their fields. Here are some clues.

Over her thirty-five years with GM, Barra, who started inspecting parts on the assembly line for Pontiac at eighteen-years old, rarely had a day when she wasn't the first to work in the morning and the last to leave at night. She wasn't merely willing to give the company her best, she was eager.

LeBron James, the greatest basketball player of his era, regularly asks for and receives a four-page scouting report on his next opponent while his teammates receive only two-page reports. Before he gets on the floor to meet that next opponent, he can tell you in extraordinary detail everything that is in that report. He is always the very last player to leave the court after each practice, staying an extra hour taking extra shots and pushing his body to unheard of limits with drill after drill.

In the in seven years of guiding his first start-up company, Mark Cuban never took a vacation. His daily habit was to read and study on new innovations in software and technology until the wee hours of every morning and then be up and ready to roll early the next day.

Tim Cook's team at Apple expects emails and texts from him beginning at 4:30 AM, and they know he will be the last one out the door each night.

Do you have the answer yet? If you think the extraordinary work ethic is the secret each of these superstars has used to reach the top then you're close, but you're not quite there yet!

The real secret is not how hard they work, but the passion that drives them to work that hard! It's not that they DO the work, it's that they LOVE the work. Hard work without passion is tedium and sooner or later will lead either to burnout or to emotionless busy-ness—it's putting in the hours without putting anything IN to the hours.

Those who are passionate about working hard put themselves on the path to servant leadership. Servant leaders do not lead by position or title. They may have them, they may not. They lead by doing whatever it takes to get things done. No job is too big, no job is too small. No job starts too early or ends too late. And do you know when you notice servant leaders the most? It's when they're not there! Suddenly, it feels as if the glue that held everything together has fallen away. That's why, when Pat Summitt passed away, virtually every single player and coach who had worked with her felt an enormous hole had been torn in their hearts. Her passion for hard work was her most powerful demonstration of how much she cared. When hard work is your passion, like Pat Summitt, you see service as love in action.

7.

DON'T JUST WORK HARD, WORK SMART.

Pat Summitt was as hard a worker as anyone who has made coaching their profession. But her legendary success and legacy are as much the result of working smart, not merely hard.

We've all heard the definition of insanity: Doing the same thing over and over again and expecting a different result. When you focus only on working hard, you may well find yourself exemplifying that definition.

Coach Summitt surrounded herself with assistant coaches who she deeply respected and who were quite willing to challenge her decisions, methods, or strategies when they thought there was a better way. If she had continued to coach exactly the same way as she did during the seven seasons when her teams lost in the Final Four, she likely never would have broken through to win eight championships. She knew she had to work smarter, not just harder.

Though at the very top of her profession, Coach Summitt constantly looked for mentors, teachers, and other coaches from whom she could learn new methods. When her fiercest rival, Geno Auriemma at UConn, rose up and changed women's basketball, winning the National Championship through their success with a different offense (called the Triple Post), Coach Summitt had two choices. Rather than stubbornly teaching her players exactly the same way she always had, she became determined to study the Triple Post intensely so she could effectively counter it.

She visited the Chicago Bulls and learned from the masters of this offense, Tex Winter and Phil Jackson. In other words, Coach Summitt made the conscious choice to work smarter, not just harder. The next season, with much the same personnel who had lost to UConn the previous season, Tennessee won the National Championship.

Warren Buffet, the Oracle of Omaha and the most successful investor in modern history, is a brilliant example of working smart and not just hard. Nearly every single day he blocks off at least a couple of hours to think, read, and study. This is sacred time, because to Buffett, if you're not learning, you're losing. He never tires of developing what he sees to be one of his greatest strengths in business—make informed rather than knee-jerk decisions.

A vital key to working smarter is to, like Warren Buffet, invest more time, effort, and focus on developing and enhancing your strengths rather than on your weaknesses. Choose to surround yourself with teammates who have strengths and passion in areas you don't and treat them with great respect and appreciation, just as Pat Summitt did with her assistant coaches.

John Wooden, the legendary UCLA basketball coach, also demonstrated a pivotal practice in working smarter, not just harder: Focus your energy on preparation. Like Coach Summit, Wooden's daily practices were filled with constant movement, repetition, and conditioning. He kept meticulous records of every drill at every practice and then studied that data diligently, looking for specific areas where he felt there were opportunities to improve. He spent four to five hours preparing for each two-hour practice.

By focusing on detailed preparation, he was able to work smarter and generate consistent improvement and powerful momentum throughout the season. As he said, "It's the little details that are vital. Little things make big things happen."

Pat Summitt used this same practice of focused and intense preparation as she tackled every challenge in her career and her life. It is little wonder that these two "Coaches of the Century" were shining examples of working smarter, not just harder.

Working harder is all about passion, effort, and energy. Working smarter is about strategy, patience, and flexibility. The combination is the stuff of legend!

8.

PUT THE TEAM
BEFORE YOURSELF

D o you know the very best thing about who you are is simply that you will do more for others than you'd do for yourself? You can only become your best when you know you are a part of a team. That is why if you don't approach each day with a passion for your team, whether your work team, family team, sports team, friend team, or community team, you'll fall short of your potential. But when you put the team before yourself, when you are more about "we" than "me," you unleash your true competitive greatness.

Coach Pat Summitt stressed that we often have no idea how much we mean to each other! We are constantly impacting our teammates through our energy, attitude, and choices. She saw this reality every single day on the basketball court. When her players put their teams before themselves, they moved faster, had more fun, were more purposeful, and performed at a higher level. This unselfish spirit was contagious and ignited positive reciprocation. Coach Summitt rewarded team-before-yourself behavior with her highest praise. She saved her most important, and sometimes severe, discipline for the opposite. In her mind, there was nothing that came before the team.

Like John Wooden, Pat passionately believed that it's amazing what can be accomplished when no one cares who gets the credit. She saw credit as something you gave while responsibility something was something you took. But she also believed that unselfishness and putting the team before yourself actually strengthened and improved you. It was not a sacrifice where you nobly gave up your glory and excellence. On the contrary, Coach Summitt knew that no one could reach their true potential as leaders and performers until they thought about more than themselves.

This fundamental belief, so much at the heart of who Pat Summitt was, was built from her first and foremost love and priority—family. When she became a parent, this belief moved from her head to her heart. Every decision she made, every action she took, became more important because she knew it would impact her son, Tyler. When he came into her life, she had a constant purpose that was bigger than herself. She believed it made her better because it inspired her to be a better example.

In his classic book, *Man's Search for Meaning*, Viktor Frankl recounted the horrors he experienced as a prisoner in the Nazi concentration camp, Auschwitz. One of the most powerful truths that Frankl discovered in the midst of this diabolical inhumanity was that though we may not have a choice in our circumstances, we always have a choice in how to react to whatever befalls us. He saw that in even the darkest moments of cruelty and pain, some of the prisoners chose to put their team of starving, beaten, and psychologically terrorized fellow inmates before themselves. Frankl wrote:

"We who lived in concentration camps can remember the men who walked through the huts comforting others, giving away their last piece of bread. They may have been few in number, but they offer sufficient proof that everything can be taken from a man but one thing: The last of human freedoms—to choose one's attitude in any given set of circumstances, to choose one's way."

These extraordinary individuals put their team before themselves and against all odds, brought a glimmer of precious hope and faith to those on the very edge of life and death. In so doing, they revealed the secret power of putting one's team before oneself: When we seek to give hope to others, to somehow help to enrich their experience, we bring purpose, meaning, and that same hope, to ourselves.

One of the great benefits of writing about the Definite Dozen is in recognizing the enormous impact of Coach Summitt's principles in my own experience. Her principle of putting the team before yourself came alive for me on one of the best days of my life, my daughter Kelsey's wedding day.

It was so extraordinary and sublime for a reason I never would have expected. You see, from the moment she took my arm to walk down that aisle, for a good six hours, I didn't think of myself once. All I could do was think of her, of her new husband Michael, of my wife Carole, and Kelsey's little sister, Jenna—my ultimate team. They tell me I was laughing and crying at the same time and I had no idea.

That day I learned what it is to truly put the team before yourself. It was the greatest feeling I have ever experienced in my life. To truly put the team before yourself is to feel the ultimate joy of unconditional love. No one understood or lived this principle more than Pat Summitt.

9.

MAKE WINNING AN ATTITUDE

What you focus on is what you create. That is why Coach Summitt believed so passionately that it was essential to make winning an attitude. She was an abundance thinker when it came to generating success. When you make winning an attitude you do not hope to win, you *know* to win. When you merely hope to win, you hold the real possibility of failure in your mind, body, and spirit in every moment. Then, when things are not going your way, it is easy to fall into the abyss because doubt has been with you all along.

But when winning becomes your attitude, you act with certainty and absolute conviction. Napoleon Hill in *Think and*

Grow Rich taught that within every adversity is planted the seed of an equivalent or greater benefit. Only when you've made winning your attitude do you focus on the potential benefit. Without that attitude, that habitual way of thinking, you will be swallowed by the adversity.

A wonderful quote by author Zig Ziglar reads, "It's your attitude, not your aptitude, that defines your altitude." Coach Summitt lived, breathed, and coached positive attitude every day. She knew that the seed of an attitude is a choice, a decision. The seed has the capacity for growth and development, but you must nurture that possibility for growth through conscious action and by developing the habit of attention, focus, and care. Once you have instilled those actions as a habit, you generate the attitude of complete confidence in your desired outcome.

And so, you plant the seed in fertile ground, you water it often, and you make sure it's getting enough sun. You don't do it once. You do it every day. You know it will sprout and grow even when you've seen no outward evidence before the stem has broken through the earth. You envision the shoot and the flowering before it happens. You know with certainty it will rise and flourish. Once it has sprouted you continue the habits of attention, focus, and care. Over time, some of the leaves and flowers turn brown. You trim them away, knowing with complete confidence that new growth will result. Choices fertilized by conscious actions become habits that lead to inner knowing, which become your constant attitudes.

Making winning an attitude requires the same process. Coach Summitt knew it was also about planting a seed, nurturing it daily, and caring for it always and in all ways.

She understood something even more powerful results when you make winning your attitude. She knew that a winning attitude was contagious when you lived it twenty-four-seven. Through a proven principle called the Pygmalion Effect, a winning attitude is transferable. The Pygmalion Effect says that our thoughts, beliefs, and expectations are magnetic and that we are actually pulling others in the direction of our thoughts about them.

When Lady Vol players and coaches look back on the experience of working with Pat Summitt, they arrive at one overwhelmingly consistent realization: Coach Summitt believed in them often more than they believed in themselves. The penetrating stare, the intense practices, the tough love, and the extraordinarily high level she demanded from her players not only on the court, but in the classroom and the community sometimes pushed these young women to the very edge of what they thought possible.

But her relentless belief in their capabilities to improve, to work harder, and to rise to their actual potential eventually took hold in their own hearts and minds. They knew she would not accept the word *can't* and that she would never give up on seeing them as champions.

Cervantes wrote in *Don Quixote*, "Too much sanity may be madness. And the maddest of all to see life as it is, and not as it should be." Pat Summitt, the ultimate positive Pygmalion, absolutely refused to see her players and coaches as less than they could be! To her it was all about attitude. And she understood how important appreciation was to a positive attitude as well. She called this her "attitude of gratitude."

As much as we are Pygmalions to others, we are equally so to ourselves. When Pat received the news that she was stricken with Early Onset Alzheimer's, her winning mindset, her power as an unstoppable positive Pygmalion rose, to meet this insidious challenge. She focused every ounce of her energy on taking constant action on what she could control and letting go of what she couldn't. She dove in to learn everything she possibly could about how she could fight the disease, counter its attacks, and execute the best possible game plan.

With passion, she worked out five days a week when she learned how effective this was in battling Alzheimer's. She diligently tackled puzzles and brain teasers to help keep her as sharp as possible. She exposed her vulnerability by coming out publicly about her diagnosis. Together with her assistant coaches, she came up with the best possible plan to organize the Lady Vol program and redistribute some of her administrative and promotional responsibilities so she could focus on what she did best, teaching and coaching her players.

Perhaps most importantly, she started the Pat Summitt Foundation to find a cure for this terrible disease. She refused to wallow in "Why me?" Instead, she stepped up with her winning attitude to say, "Why not me?" She wanted to help everyone she could to deal with Alzheimer's and make the most of every precious moment.

Pat Summitt's winning attitude taught us all to move from fear to freedom and from failure to faith.

10.

BE A COMPETITOR

I f there is one word that more than any other described Pat Summitt, it was the word competitor. She absolutely loved the challenge of competition. It was not just the winning that Coach Summitt loved (and she did love winning!), it was the power of competition to bring out one's best and, in turn, to elevate others to do the same.

In a very real sense Coach Summitt understood that her fiercest competitors were in many ways her most important teammates. They raised the bar for her players, coaches, and herself. Their excellence ignited Coach Summitt to never become complacent and to always strive to get better.

To Pat Summitt, being a competitor was not about innate talent. It was about playing hard, about effort, attitude, and energy. To her, it was about heart, not ability. Because of that simple truth, being a competitor depended upon controlling what you could control—your choices. Coach Summitt loved competition so passionately because though she knew her players' gifts came from God. Their grit was 100% their choice. This was the area in which she believed she could have a real impact as a coach. Her competitive nature meant that she would use every tool, trick, and technique to motivate her players and coaches to hustle and fight with every ounce of their spirit. She also went on record to share that she would pursue a recruit who demonstrated incredible heart and competitive spirit over a player with great talent but a less passionate, competitive posture.

At the very core of being a competitor is irrepressible resiliency. Often, you have very little control of when you get knocked down. However, almost always you have complete control of getting back up. Resiliency is the choice to turn challenge into opportunity, loss into learning, and injury into inspiration.

Growing up on the farm with three older brothers and an intimidating father, Pat Summitt wasn't treated like a baby sister but rather as the little brother whose job it was to get picked on and often bullied. When she grew older and became a basketball player, it was obvious that although she was talented, her strong suit on the court was less about pure talent and more about her unstoppable energy and guts. Even later, as a coach who got knocked down seven times in the Final Four before breaking through and winning eight National Championships, Pat Summitt was the quintessential competitor. The word *can't* was not in her vocabulary.

When stricken with early onset Alzheimer's, Coach Summitt was once again the ultimate competitor. Instead of dwelling on her illness, she focused on how she could use her example, energy, and competitive spirit to fight the disease and do all she could to help accelerate the finding of a cure. At the 2012 ESPY Awards, Pat Summitt received the most prestigious and important award of all, the Arthur Ashe Courage Award. She was honored that night for her head-on approach to battling Alzheimer's.

But the deeper, more lasting, and more profound reason for the moving tribute she received was the incalculable impact her competitive spirit has had on women's basketball, all of women's sports, the advancement of women, equality, and of humanity. Sally Jenkins, Pulitzer Prize nominee, explained Coach Summitt's approach to transformation perfectly when she said, "She didn't try to take off her high heel and smash it through the glass ceiling. She was a glass-cutter, etching it over and over, a little deeper each time."

Jenkins continued to explain that in so doing, Pat won everyone's respect until that ceiling simply no longer made any sense. In reality, she ignited women well beyond the confines of sport to do the same, to have the courage and energy to compete in fields long dominated by men.

Reese Witherspoon narrated the magnificent tribute film about Pat that night at the ESPY's. A long-time fan of Coach Summitt and the Lady Vols, the Academy Award Winning actress drew upon the example of Coach Summitt in her own career. She has used that inspiration to cut through glass many thought impenetrable, producing movies that featured strong leading roles for women.

When she first began her film career, Reese was cast in dramatic roles. Casting directors immediately pigeon-holed her and assumed she had no comedic chops. But, like Pat Summitt, being told she couldn't do something was a sure-fire way to ignite her competitive spirit. And so, Reese landed the role of Elle Woods in *Legally Blonde*. That glass began to weaken just a bit.

Her enormous success as a comedic actress however, didn't open more doors, but rather just rerouted her into a new pigeon-hole. Winning the Oscar for her powerful performance in *Walk the Line* was a tremendous achievement and an unforgettable moment in her career, but it was fleeting. Older producers and directors began to question Reese could still sell enough tickets as a glamourous romantic star. What's more, there simply were not movies being made with true leading roles for women. As Reese put it, "By lead, I don't mean the wife of the lead or the girlfriend of the lead. I mean the lead, the hero of the story."

This was the moment when Reese's ambition and determination to be a competitor ignited a change in the status quo. This change is revolutionizing the film industry, just as Pat Summitt revolutionized sports. Reese envisioned a whole new cinema industry with just as many successful, money-making, and critically acclaimed movies centered on powerful leading roles for women as are for men. She realized that since no one had done it before, she'd have to figure out how to do it herself. Reese started her own film production company, Pacific Standard Films, risking her own money in the start-up venture, with the clear and powerful mission to tell stories about women.

Forty years before Reese produced her first movie, Pat Summitt began her journey. Pat's journey would give ambitious women leaders like Reese Witherspoon hope and illuminate a way forward that was lit with possibility.

When Coach Summitt coached her first game at the University of Tennessee, she knew that if things were going to get done, she was going to have to do them! There simply wasn't anyone else to shoulder that responsibility. Here's how she described that first game as the brand new, twenty-two-year-old head coach of the University of Tennessee Lady Vols: "The day of our first game arrived: December 7th, 1974, against Mercer University. I got to Alumni Gym early because, in addition to doing the team laundry, it was my responsibility to see that the floor was ready... I turned on the lights and found the game clock and set it up. I swept the floor clean. Next, I had to set up the benches... Once the floor was set up, I went into the locker room, which was just a lounge area with a couple of vending machines and some straight-backed Naugahyde chairs. I began to tape our player's ankles, which I wasn't very good at—in our first practice, I left ridges in the tape, which rubbed against their feet and blistered them. Thirty years later players still complained that they had scars from my tape job."

When she took the position as head coach, she had no idea that the job description included custodian, set-up crew, laundress, van driver, ticket promoter, team manager, and trainer. But when you are a competitor you do whatever it takes to get things done. No job is too big or too little. No job starts too early or ends too late.

Following in Pat Summitt's trailblazing footsteps, Reese plunged headfirst into the pursuit of her dream with an irrepressible, competitive spirit. She described those first steps when she delivered the keynote address to an enthralled room full of young women at the Glamour Magazine Women of the Year Awards:

"Female ambition is not a trait to fear. Instead we should wholeheartedly embrace it. I'm a very avid reader. In fact, I'm a complete book nerd. So is my producing partner, so we tore through tons of manuscripts and read so many things before they were published. But we could only find two pieces of material that we thought were right. We optioned them with our own money, and we prayed that they would work. Both had strong, complicated, fascinating women at the center, and both were written by women. And lo and behold, both books hit number one on the *New York Times* bestsellers list. One was called *Gone Girl* and the second was called *Wild*. So, we made those two films last year, and those two films rose to over a half a billion dollars worldwide, and we got three Academy Award nominations for women in acting performances."

Reese's company went on to produce the enormously successful *Big Little Lies*, television mini-series, which won eight Emmy's in 2017. True competitors like Pat Summitt and Reese Witherspoon are not short-term thinkers, but rather long-term winners who change their world. Reese finished her speech with words Pat Summitt lived every day as the ultimate competitor.

"What is it in life that you think you can't accomplish? Or what is it that people have said you cannot do? Wouldn't it feel really good to prove them all wrong? Because I believe ambition is not a dirty word. It's just believing in yourself and your abilities. Imagine this: What would happen if we were all brave enough to be a little bit more ambitious? I think the world would change."

11.

CHANGE IS A MUST

What's the best thing that has ever happened to you in your life? Was it graduating high school or college? Was it getting that first, important job? Was it getting married, the birth of your children, or breaking through and accomplishing something you didn't know you could do? There's something surprising about every one of these wonderful events. Every one of them was a change and a disruption of your status quo!

And yet, what is your immediate reaction to change? Is it fear, worry, doubt, or dread? Do you push back against change and hold tight to the past? Do you actively seek change or prefer to deal with it only when there seems to be no escape? Do you focus on the possibility in change or the uncertainty? Do you thrive on change or merely survive it?

You might think that Coach Summitt, one of the most disciplined, consistent, ritualistic, organized, and successful leaders ever, was steadfast and stubborn about staying the course. You might assume she chose to stick with methods that had proved tried and true under fire. However, she was absolutely committed and determined to change. She believed that unless she disrupted the status quo, she could easily find herself mired in quicksand. Pat Summitt didn't just accept change, she believed that change was a must. She also believed that each of us needed to be a catalyst for change when change was necessary.

Quite simply, she knew it was her attitude about change that would determine the altitude she'd attain in her life. Before Coach Summitt won her first of eight National Championships, she was viewed by many as a very good coach who just couldn't win the big one! That's a far cry from the legendary status she holds today. It was only because she embraced change and saw it as a must that she broke through to her historic level.

Again, humility is crucial if we are to become change leaders. Remember, it's been wisely said that humility isn't thinking less of yourself, it's thinking of yourself less. We must believe there is always more to learn and always the opportunity to find a better way. We must always be open to changing our approach, decisions, and actions.

When we shoot a rocket to the moon it does not travel in a straight line. It moves teleologically. In other words, it changes and adjusts according to feedback in much the same way that if we held the steering wheel in our car dead still, we'd end up in a ditch. Only when we decide that change is a must will we move beyond the definition of insanity: Doing the same thing over and over again and expecting a different result.

One of Pat Summitt's great friends and admirers was the Duke University and United States Men's Olympic team coaching giant, Mike Krzyzewski. Coach K considered Pat Summitt one of the greatest coaches of all time. When, in 2018, he surpassed Coach Summitt's record for the most career wins in any collegiate sport he said, "The lady who had that record would have won hundreds more. Pat Summitt was as good of a coach as there was."

Coach K shared Pat Summitt's conviction that change is a must. It was one of the most powerful principles they had in common. When faced with the challenge of UConn's Triple Post offense, Coach Summitt embraced change to learn all she could to counter the challenge. Her humility and willingness to change led to several more championship trophies for the Lady Vols.

In the 1990s, Mike Krzyzewski was strongly opposed to recruiting players to Duke who were likely to jump to the NBA after one season. He, like Pat Summitt and John Wooden, considered himself first and foremost a teacher. He believed he coached players as people even more than as basketball players, and the thought of only working with and developing his players for one season was distasteful and discouraging to him. So, although he had a handful of his players leave Duke for the NBA after their freshmen seasons between 1999 and 2013, most of his teams featured upper classmen who had paid their dues and grown under his tutelage both in their basketball skills and leadership.

The one-and-done phenomenon grew into the norm in men's college basketball, driven by the NBA age entry rules, a dramatic increase in publicity and visibility of high school basketball stars, and even more by a changing mindset among these young athletes who now approached college as a one-year training camp. Coach K realized he could either change and adapt or stubbornly hold on to his old ways.

Through his years as the US National and Olympic Team head coach, Krzyzewski built tremendous relationships with the finest NBA superstars such as LeBron James, Kevin Durant, Carmelo Anthony, and Stephen Curry. Like Coach Summitt, always humble, Coach K not only led USA Basketball, he learned from these elite players, several of whom had either gone directly from high school into the NBA or had been one-and-done college players. He saw firsthand the quality of their character, their intense work ethic, their passion for teamwork, and their genuine unselfishness. Coach K saw that these superstars had followed the streamlined path to the professional ranks and could become such outstanding leaders and teammates. He realized that as long as he believed players were coachable, hungry to learn, and team oriented, he could embrace change and enthusiastically recruit players to Duke he knew were likely to leave after one year.

He decided, as Pat Summitt so consistently taught, that change was a must. In virtually every field of human endeavor, from sports, to business, to media, to communication, and to education, the constant and growing challenge is to do more with less. Instead of focusing on the three years he would no longer be able to coach his recruits, he decided to do everything he could to impact them as players and people in the one year he did have.

In 2014 Duke won the National Championship with three freshman starters who moved on to the NBA after that championship season. For the remainder of his legendary career, Coach K was a phenomenal recruiter of high school stars who are very likely to follow the one-and-done path to the NBA. As Pat Summitt had modeled in her career through humility, wisdom, awareness, and flexibility, you can thrive on change and transform challenge into championships.

12.

HANDLE SUCCESS LIKE YOU HANDLE FAILURE

Although Pat Summitt hated to lose, she also saw failure as vital to the improvement process. After all, as John Wooden often said, "Failure is never fatal. Success is never final." Pat Summitt believed that it's what you learn and apply from every experience and performance that truly matters. The essential focus in her teaching and coaching was to control what is controllable—effort, energy, attitude, and putting the team first.

So, whether Tennessee came out ahead or behind on the scoreboard, whether or not they won the National Championship, Coach Summitt always felt there were areas to improve, adjustments to make, and lessons to learn. As a result, she was sometimes much more disappointed in her team after a win than a loss if she felt her players had fallen below their potential and come out on top simply because of superior talent.

When you handle success like you handle failure, you keep perspective and balance. You approach every experience as a leg of a journey rather than as a final destination. You never become arrogant or conceited no matter how much success you have achieved because you recognize that change is the only constant. Unless you learn as much from your successes as you do from your failures you will be unable to improve.

Coach Pat Summitt believed in disrupting the status quo long before those became buzz words in personal and team development. She sought to shape the future rather than to wait for it. With this perspective, it was natural for her to become a life-long learner who recognized that each day we're given the greatest gift of all, which is called *today*. Every day is new with new challenges, opportunities, successes, and failures. To overblow successes or to hold on to failures was simply counter-productive. This type of mindset placed your focus on the past rather than the present, which is where the only real progress can be achieved.

The story of the great American track star, Wilma Rudolph, provides a brilliant demonstration of this Definite Dozen principle. Wilma showed what is possible when you handle success and failure with the same indomitable spirit. Rudolph won three gold medals at the 1960 Rome Olympics, including the coveted one-hundred-meter dash crown, earning her the title of the World's Fastest Woman. But it was the way she dealt with failure long before she stood atop that Olympic medal stand that led to her incredible success.

Wilma was born into extreme poverty in rural Tennessee, the twentieth of twenty-two children. She was stricken with many diseases as a young child—scarlet fever, double pneumonia, and most debilitating, polio, which left her left leg and foot terribly weak and increasingly deformed. But little Wilma's spirit knew no limits. When her mother asked her what she wanted to become when she grew up, Wilma told her that she wanted to be the fastest runner in the world. The polio was cruel, however, and by the time she was eight-years-old the doctors informed her mother that Wilma would never walk again.

Wilma's mother, Blanche Rudolph, refused to accept that crippling life sentence for her daughter. For two straight years, twice each week, she brought Wilma to Meharry Hospital—the black medical college of Fisk University in Nashville—a difficult trek of fifty miles each way, for treatment and physical therapy. After two years, Wilma had made enough progress that she could walk with the aid of a metal brace. For another two years, her mother, brothers, and sisters helped Wilma with physical therapy exercises at home every single day. They never gave up. By thirteen, Wilma could walk without the brace, crutches, or corrective shoes.

That's when she decided to transform her six-years-old vision of becoming a great runner into reality. Nothing was going to keep her from running! At thirteen-years-old she competed in her first school one-hundred-meter race and finished dead last. For that first year of sprinting, that was the only place she finished—last.

But rather than becoming discouraged, she used each race as an opportunity to learn, to improve, and to persevere. She made no excuses. And gradually, she got faster, and faster, and faster, until she earned a track scholarship to Tennessee State University. From there she just kept right on running, earning a spot on the 1956 US Olympic team and a silver medal in the Melbourne Games. Four years later, in Rome, she became the fastest woman on planet earth and the greatest female sprinter in history up to that time.

When Wilma won her Olympic gold medals, she handled success as she had handled failure, just the way Pat Summitt handled the diagnosis of Alzheimer's, with grace and humility. She said, "Always remember, no matter what you may accomplish in life, someone always helps you. Winning is great, sure, but if you are really going to do something in life, the secret is learning how to lose. Nobody goes undefeated all the time. If you can pick up after a crushing defeat, and go on to win again, you are going to be a champion someday."

Jack Nicklaus is considered by many to have been the greatest golfer of all time. He won eighteen major championships, and only Tiger Woods, with fourteen major victories, is within seven of that remarkable achievement. Perhaps just as extraordinary, Nicklaus finished second in nineteen major championships! After every single one of those runner-up finishes, Jack Nicklaus was the epitome of class, dignity, and respect. He always gave tremendous praise to the champion. He never made excuses for coming up short, and without exception, gave credit while taking responsibility for his own performance. When he won, he was equally respectful of his competitors and genuinely grateful for his good fortune in being able to come out on top.

Like Jack Nicklaus, Wilma Rudolph, and Pat Summitt, those who handle success like they handle failure are very hard to offend. They appreciate their competitors and realize that, in a very real sense, they are special teammates who challenge and push them to bring out their best. They accept responsibility when their efforts are not quite enough to come out victorious. They are never defensive and never blame others or make excuses.

In her first seven trips to the Final Four, Pat Summitt never achieved her dream of making it all the way to the top. But by handling success and failure equally, by looking at setbacks and disappointments as steps that brought her ever closer to success, she was able to learn, improve, and ultimately triumph, with eight National Championships.

13.

INTRODUCTION TO A LEGEND: JOHN WOODEN

For most of my life I followed John Wooden's career as a coach and a leader. It had been my dream to spend some time with him and get to know him since I was twelve-years-old growing up in Southern California. He always embodied integrity and class. His mild demeanor, humility, and graciousness were so genuine one might forget that he accomplished more in the highly competitive field of Men's NCAA Basketball than anyone before or after him.

In his final twelve years at UCLA, John Wooden's teams won a staggering total of ten National Championships. No other men's coach in history has won more than five. When he retired in 1975 he was the only individual to be elected to the College

Basketball Hall of Fame as both a player and a coach. He was truly one of a kind, a true legend.

Yet, it was not so much *what* Coach Wooden accomplished that was the true measure of his greatness. It was *how* he achieved his success. As unparalleled as his basketball record was in the men's game, he was an even better husband and father. John Wooden, like Pat Summitt, always remembered that he coached people first, basketball second. Both of these legends understood that whether your arena is athletics, business, education, or parenting, the most important focus of your energy is ultimately on the human spirit.

In every interaction I had with Coach Wooden I was determined to be a sponge—to soak in everything I could about his basic philosophies, beliefs, and strategies. For more than thirty years I have been passionate about sharing that golden information with others. Since he passed away in 2010 at the age of ninety-nine, that passion has only grown stronger. Coach Wooden's teaching is more important than ever. Each of us has the opportunity to powerfully and positively impact our families, work teams, and communities. By modeling the examples of legends like Coach Wooden and Coach Summitt, we gain insights and understanding that will help us become increasingly successful in our careers and our lives.

John Wooden loved poetry and philosophical quotations. He attached so much meaning to these verses and statements of principle, that together, they portray a sense of his true character. There is perhaps no better way to understand his genius and example than through these quotes. They enable us to discover that the foundational beliefs that guided John Wooden's remarkable life are clear, simple, and readily available to emulate and internalize. By modeling his wisdom, you, too, can become the leader you were put on this earth to be! John Wooden said, "True happiness comes from the things that can't be taken away."

My dream of meeting Coach Wooden came true when he graciously invited me to visit him in his apartment for an interview. I was preparing to write my first book, *Beyond Success*, based on his *Pyramid of Success*. When I walked into his living room, everywhere I looked were photographs of family—children, grandchildren, and great-grandchildren. Conspicuously absent were the countless awards he had received over the years. Indeed, the trophies that had real meaning for him were his mementos from his family and friends...and his books. He was a ravenous reader with scores of books of poetry, novels, biographies, and spiritual volumes stuffing his shelves.

As I looked around me during that first meeting with Coach Wooden, I began to understand what made him so unique and extraordinary. I had never met a man who was as clear and centered about his priorities as John Wooden. The more we talked, the more I realized that he had internalized and affirmed the principles that guided him by repeating these bits of philosophy every single day. He repeated these in the form of his poems, quotes, and creeds. He shared these ideas with others the way most of us talk about the weather. He never stopped teaching.

The cornerstone of his philosophy was a simple, seven-point creed given to him by his father the day John Wooden graduated from his one-room country grade school. Coach carried the creed with him in one form or another from that day forward:

- Be true to yourself.
- Make each day your masterpiece.
- Help others.
- Drink deeply from good books, especially the Bible.
- Make friendship a fine art.
- Build a shelter against a rainy day.
- Pray for guidance; count and give thanks for your blessings every day.

This creed quite accurately defined the essence of the way John Wooden lived his life. To exemplify this creed is to move swiftly and purposefully along the pathway to lasting success.

When I asked Coach Wooden about his strategic approach to a season, to daily practice sessions, and to games, balance and preparation were the two overriding themes. He was a long-term thinker who used the short-term to fine-tune his strategy. Three of his favorite quotes illustrated this focus:

- "Failure to prepare is preparing to fail."
- "Be quick, but never hurry."
- "Learn as if you were to live forever; live as if you were to die tomorrow."

Coach Wooden's practice during the off-season demonstrated his dedication to preparation and constant improvement. As soon as the college season ended, he selected a single topic to study in great depth throughout the off-season. In his earlier years, he chose physical or strategic aspects of the game of basketball such as rebounding, fast break offense, or zone defense.

In later years, he shifted to more psychological elements of the sport, such as pre-game mental preparation or visualization. He then devoured every piece of information he could find about his selected topic. He interviewed fellow coaches to uncover fine details that enhanced his knowledge and understanding. There was simply no satisfying his voracious appetite for learning.

Not one to collect content to simply gather the information, he went much further and constructed a composite of the most important distinctions he accumulated from his study. By engaging and applying himself creatively in this way, he became much better prepared to teach the new methods effectively. He understood that mastery requires proactive involvement rather than passive study.

Coach Wooden's commitment to lifelong learning stemmed from his humility. He always knew there was more to discover. One of my personal favorite John Wooden common-sense quotes summed up his uncommon humility: "It's what you learn after you know everything that makes the difference."

In the long run, those who constantly look for finer and finer distinctions and then use their increased knowledge and understanding as teachers, coaches, and business leaders, will soar to the tops of their fields. Coach profoundly said, "Success accompanies attention to little details. It is this that makes for difference between champion and near champion."

Coach Wooden considered his ability to organize practices as one of his primary strengths. He was known for running practices that were relatively short and meticulously planned. Every moment of every practice involved movement and clear purpose. Practices started and ended on time. Players moved in units from drill to drill with a consistent emphasis on repetition, repetition, repetition. He knew that only by practicing fundamentals constantly and with great concentration would good judgement and precision execution become automatic.

Over the years he became convinced that every detail was important. A classic example of this extraordinary attention to detail was his annual training session on *socks*. Coach Wooden believed that no player was better than their feet. If players developed blisters or sores, they would slow down at crucial moments. They would unconsciously begin to compensate in their movement and increase the chance of injury to their knees or hips. Consequently, each season he gave his players a detailed, step-by-step tutorial on the proper way to put on their socks so they would avoid the wrinkles that led to blisters. His remarkable attention to detail made a lasting, positive impact on his players. They knew that if there was a competitive edge to be gained, their coach would find it.

Coach Wooden made it a must to end each workout on a positive note. In every practice there would be ups and downs, just as there are in each day. He recognized that what you focus on determines your attitude. Many people cling to the negative or painful experiences in each day. For example, if they had forty things happen in that day and thirty-nine were good to great, but one was a downer, the tendency for many was to focus on that one negative and forget about all the positives. By ending every practice on an upbeat note, Coach Wooden trained his players to positively anticipate their next workout. He understood the truth that the last impression of today is the first impression of tomorrow.

John Wooden was extremely dedicated to integrating the day-to-day progress of his team. He kept personal notebooks that he updated daily. One contained detailed statistical records of his team's performance. The other was a listing of all the drills and practices his players had completed during the season. These notebooks enabled Coach Wooden to tell you what his players did during any practice from 1949 to 1975. He could clearly detail each player's statistics from every practice during that span.

But far more important than recording this information was his regular practice of using it to improve. He examined and assessed these records every day in his preparation for practices and games. His practice sessions changed dramatically from when he began at UCLA in 1948 until he retired in 1975. However, the changes from year to year were subtle. It was through his dedication to measuring, recording, assessing, and integrating that he was able to continually improve.

Like Pat Summitt, he was constantly focused on putting the team before oneself. He often said, "It's amazing how much can be accomplished when no one cares who gets the credit." Perhaps more than any other, this quote captures the heart of John Wooden's vision of a team centered around unselfishness, camaraderie, communication, and united purpose.

Coach Wooden's UCLA squads were the epitome of this team concept. His beliefs concerning team began with a core conviction: "A man may make mistakes, but he isn't a failure until he starts blaming someone else." Blaming others takes focus away from the one element in human performance that you control—you. It dissipates energy and destroys teamwork.

This same tenet is true in a family, a business, and within yourself. John Wooden thrived on accepting the responsibility for his teams in good times and in bad. He taught his players to embrace their responsibility to themselves and their team. To Coach Wooden, personal responsibility was a fundamental gift from God.

Wooden taught that every member of the unit played an essential role, from the players, to the coaches, trainers, and student managers. Unselfishness was a trait he absolutely insisted upon. To him, the greatest privilege his athletes had was to practice, and the next was to play in the games. If a player put himself before the team, he would remove those privileges. He often said that the bench was sometimes a coach's best friend.

When asked to characterize what made for a great team player, he thought carefully about his answer and replied: "All of the great team players at UCLA were different in many ways. Yet in one way they were the same. Each drove himself to be the best he could be—always in relation to the team. They weren't motivated by individual statistics or awards. The only credit they truly valued was credit for the team."

In his early years as an English teacher and coach, John Wooden set about organizing his principles and philosophies into a simple structure that would become the foundation of his teaching. Like the ancient Egyptian Pyramids, Coach Wooden's *Pyramid of Success* was built block by block to be solid, strong, and eternal. The success one could achieve through exemplifying each block was not about trying to be the best but about becoming your best. It was not about comparing yourself to others but rather about consistently moving toward achieving your own potential.

When Coach Wooden sadly left us just short of his one-hundredth birthday, he had achieved the success he considered worth striving for: Peace of mind from the self-satisfaction in knowing that he'd given the best of which he was capable. He, like Pat Summitt after him, left this world a better place. He brought us belief that we can choose faith over fear, freedom over failure, and we-go over ego. Now it's time for the principles of the *Pyramid of Success* to live on through each of us.

14.

COACH WOODEN'S PYRAMID OF SUCCESS: INDUSTRIOUSNESS

Like Pat Summitt, John Wooden grew up on a farm where there were no days off, no excuses, and no laziness allowed. Young Johnny Wooden rose early each morning and put in a couple of hours of hard, physical work before he went off to his one-room country schoolhouse. From an early age, chores and then homework had to be completed before any basketball or baseball could be played. Farm life was simple, clear, and straightforward. It was here that John Wooden learned that there are simply no shortcuts to excellence and no replacement for industriousness.

It was on the farm that Wooden also began to understand the rewards and enormous benefits of industriousness. With hard work came focus, direction, clarity, and the quiet confidence that can only come when you walk your talk and deliver consistently on your responsibilities and duties. Industriousness requires self-discipline and remaining true to your priorities. Most of all, the habit of industriousness required by life on the farm taught John Wooden that though he could not control the snow, rain, sunshine, or crop prices, he *could* control his effort, energy, and attitude, even in the midst of great adversity.

This became a central theme of his extraordinary life—the conviction that real success was completely based upon controlling what you could control and focusing not on the result but rather on what you put in to every undertaking. It was through the lifelong habits of industriousness he developed on the farm that John Wooden's definition of success was born: Success is peace of mind that comes from knowing you've given the best of which you're capable.

It was Coach Wooden's passion for industriousness that led him to make it one of the two cornerstones of his *Pyramid of Success*. Its position in the Pyramid is crucial, for without solid cornerstones there can be no support for the rest of the structure. Without a solid foundation built from repetition and industriousness, there can be no mastery.

Just as Pat Summitt taught her players at the University of Tennessee to work smart, not just hard, Coach Wooden believed that industriousness must be centered on three key areas to be truly effective: Preparation, balance, and presence.

John Wooden ran some of the shortest practices in college basketball, yet his players were incredibly conditioned and seemed to rise to their highest level as the season wore on. How did he do this? The secret was in his preparation. He meticulously studied his notebooks filled with statistics and detailed descriptions of prior practices and performances on every player. He used that information to plan, adjust, and improve.

Wooden spent much more time planning daily practices than running them. That level of preparation and planning meant that every single second during practice was filled with movement, focus, and purpose. There was no sitting idly at Wooden's practices. They were like three ring circuses with every player fully engaged in drills, exercises, or game simulations, nonstop. As he often said, "Failure to prepare is preparing to fail."

Wooden believed in hard work, but not workaholism. His long-term perspective enabled him to realize that when industriousness was thrown out of balance, the ultimate result would be burnout, mental and emotional fatigue, and often, resentment. For two hours each day at practice he wanted his team to be: Completely focused as UCLA basketball players and fully present for the task at hand, for instruction, and for their teammates. For the other twenty-two hours each day he wanted them to focus on the other important aspects of their young lives…their studies, families, friends, and faith. He consistently taught that only balanced industriousness and full presence keeps you fresh, energized, and able to perform at your best.

Coach Wooden valued extraordinary industriousness as much as any other principle in his Pyramid of Success. He held a very special place in his heart for his players who demonstrated that little bit of extra hustle, who just wouldn't quit no matter what obstacles they encountered, and who never complained and seemed to love hard work.

He said, "Players with fight never lose a game, they just run out of time." Wooden's greatest hero, his father, was exactly that kind of example of unselfish industriousness. And so, when Wooden coached some of these players who may not have been blessed with the most natural talent, he believed that their industriousness and mental toughness would drive them to achieve their potential and overcome obstacles, perhaps more than those who had a much easier road.

Pat Summitt also had a special affinity for industriousness, as demonstrated by her Definite Dozen principle: Make hard work a passion. So many of her players came from those who are perhaps the greatest examples of industriousness in our society—single mothers and grandmothers. All-time great Lady Vols including Daedra Charles, Bridgette Gordon, Chamique Holdsclaw, Tamika Catchings, Semeka Randall, and Holly Warlick learned industriousness from their single moms or grandmothers. Their caretakers often worked two and three jobs, seven days a week, to make ends meet.

The young women Coach Summitt recruited into her program, many of them black, had not had an easy road and had been raised by women who had it even tougher. Summitt had a unique appeal to these women and shared a very special understanding with them. They sent their daughters to learn from her because she knew what it was to raise a child and keep up a home while also being the chief breadwinner in the household.

Coach Summitt truly honored the work of these industrious single moms. She both admired and related to their selfless grind and utter devotion to do whatever they could to help their daughters grow into strong, self-sufficient, hard-working women. She learned of the grace and dignity that comes from unselfish industriousness first-hand, from her own mother Hazel. She watched her mother cook, clean, wash, work the fields, milk cows, drive the trucks, work at the store, and then come home and feed her husband and five children after having worked twice as hard and done twice as much as anyone in the house. She watched her mother do this day after day, week after week, and year after year.

The greatness of these two Coaches of the Century, John Wooden and Pat Summitt, was rooted in the lessons they learned from family, farm life, and faith, that a life well-lived begins with devoted industriousness.

15.

ENTHUSIASM

The other cornerstone at the foundation of the *Pyramid of Success* is enthusiasm. Again, this position in the Pyramid is vital. Industriousness without enthusiasm can become tedious, burdensome, and heavy. Enthusiasm without industriousness leads to unfulfilled potential. The combination is unstoppable.

When I first met Coach Wooden I asked him, "Coach, what's the difference between a good team and a great one?" His answer pinpointed the importance of enthusiasm.

He said, "Most people believe that the difference between good and great is determined by talent. But after a lifetime of working with people, I believe there are no overachievers. We are all underachievers. We have no idea of what is truly inside of us, of how blessed we are. The pursuit of excellence is seeking to develop our own potential. When it comes down to it, the difference between good teams and great ones is the same difference between good and great teachers, coaches, leaders, and parents. The difference comes down to two words. Good teams are willing…great teams are *eager*."

When you are eager, you are brimming with enthusiasm. You are motivated not from a feeling of have to, but rather from a feeling of want to, like to, love to, and can't wait to! What's more, true enthusiasm must be more about the journey than the destination, or you're highly unlikely to ever reach that destination.

Enthusiasm is born of optimism and faith. You choose to believe you can always improve and that there is always more to learn. Indeed, it is the love of learning that fuels enthusiasm, for it fires your spirit to always seek to be the best of which you're capable.

Coach Wooden had an undending passion for teaching. In fact, he never called himself a coach. He always considered himself a teacher. His constant enthusiasm was directed at three primary targets: People, fundamentals, and change.

Here is a magnificent truth about human beings…we are at our best when we are in service to others. As one of Coach Wooden's greatest heroes, Mother Teresa put it, "Service is love in action." When you are enthusiastic about people, your great joy and fulfillment comes from helping them grow closer to their potential. Whenever you seek to enrich another person's experience, you can't help but enrich your own.

For some, the word fundamentals conjures up dull, basic, drudgery. There's not a lot of glitz and glamour attached to fundamentals. But until you become highly proficient in the fundamentals of your craft, you cannot achieve excellence. Without enthusiasm for fundamentals, you'll give up or lose interest before true mastery is possible. When you have great enthusiasm about fundamentals, you thrive on repetition. Like Coach Wooden, you love practices every bit as much, or even more than, the games because you know that that is where real improvement is generated.

Perhaps the most important focus of his enthusiasm, and the most surprising, was on change. The truth is that most of us fight change, or at minimum, have a gut reaction to push against change. Coach Wooden proactively sought change. He was eager to challenge and disrupt the status quo. He was much more interested in learning and improving than in having to be right. Coach Wooden believed that we can only approach our greatest potential when we are filled with enthusiasm about learning.

Oprah Winfrey's triumphant rags-to-riches story is a shining testimony to the power of this kind of irrepressible enthusiasm about lifelong learning. The daughter of a low-income, teenage mother, Oprah spent her first years being raised by her maternal grandmother in rural Mississippi. At six-years-old she was sent to live with her mother and two brothers in an inner-city, Milwaukee neighborhood where she was surrounded by poverty and ignorance. Beginning at the age of nine, she was sexually abused by her uncle, cousin, and a family friend. At fourteen, she gave birth to a son, who died shortly after he was born.

The odds of her breaking free from such oppressive conditions seemed terribly low. But despite her circumstances, a flame of enthusiasm burned within her throughout her difficult childhood. This flame fueled her belief that more was possible for her in life and that she could somehow rise higher than anyone believed. She didn't know where it came from and she couldn't put the feeling into words. But that flame would not go out.

At fourteen, shortly after losing her son, Oprah was sent to live with her father in Nashville, Tennessee. Vernon Winfrey, though very strict, had one area of unbridled enthusiasm, one area of commitment that was absolute: His passion for education. As John Wooden saw with his players and coaches, enthusiasm is contagious. Vernon's love of learning took hold in young Oprah and gave purpose, discipline, and direction to her enthusiasm. For the first time, she not only believed she was going somewhere in her life, she began to see a destination. Education provided Oprah with a GPS. She earned a scholarship to Tennessee State University where she discovered her passion for a career in media and journalism.

Her enthusiasm for learning and personal growth transformed Oprah's belief about setbacks and obstacles. To her, they were no longer failures, they were opportunities to discover fresh insights, open new possibilities, and move forward in new ways. As Napoleon Hill wrote in *Think and Grow Rich*: "Within every adversity is planted the seed of an equivalent or greater benefit." When you are filled with enthusiasm, you immediately look for the benefit. Without enthusiasm, you are swallowed alive by the adversity.

Oprah's boundless enthusiasm led her to build the Harpo Productions empire and to impact hundreds of millions of people in extraordinary ways. She used her iconic position as perhaps the most influential woman on earth to ignite countless people to get excited about reading, personal growth, and making a difference. She made generosity the ultimate "cool," and pioneered a whole new phenomenon in daytime television called "edutainment" that both entertained and educated her enormous viewing audience. Like John Wooden and Pat Summitt, she helped the world see that with enthusiasm, astonishing things are possible, especially when you pay it forward!

16.

FRIENDSHIP, LOYALTY, AND COOPERATION

The three blocks in the center of the Pyramid's base, friendship, loyalty, and cooperation, are placed at such foundational positions because John Wooden, just like Pat Summitt, always believed that he coached people first, basketball second. All the physical talent in the world meant little if his players didn't develop the key elements of these three interconnected blocks. Together, they generate the heartbeat of synergy, chemistry, and teamwork. He deeply believed that human beings can only be at their best when they work well with others.

With a kindly twinkle in his eye, Coach Wooden occasionally said, "There were a few of my players I didn't particularly like, but there wasn't a single one I didn't love." To Coach Wooden, real friends don't always tell you what you want to hear. But they always tell you what they believe you need to hear. Thus, friendship is built from mutual respect and concern rather than style and attraction. And so, it is long-term and solid.

To John Wooden, friendship was driven by a passion to serve. And as one of his heroes, Mother Teresa, said, "Service is love in action."

Coach also believed that whenever we seek to enrich another person's experience, we can't help but enrich our own. In other words, friendship makes both of us better and creates the kind of synergy where one plus one can equal fifty.

John Wooden looked at loyalty in much the same way he looked at credit. It is something you give freely, not something you take or demand. Like Pat Summitt, he believed you build loyalty by being loyal. At the very center of his loyalty block was his lifelong conviction that human beings will do more for others than they'll do for themselves. Being loyal gives you a purpose that is bigger than yourself. And so, loyalty is absolutely pivotal if a team is to come together and rise to their potential. When loyalty abounds, energy soars.

Real loyalty shines brightest during the toughest times. When you hold firm to your support for your teammates when things are not going well, making mistakes, and not performing at their best, they are far more likely to do the same for you when you are going through similar valleys.

Most of all, Coach Wooden believed in being loyal to one's own core values, beliefs, and standards. Without the foundation of being true to your own word, your true character, he believed it would be far more likely that your loyalty to others would waiver when tempted by personal gain or advantage.

As an eighteen-year-old basketball phenomenon and the most highly recruited player in the nation, during that time of highly charged civil rights tension, Lou Alcindor chose UCLA. He felt that out west in the hip, Hollywood world of Southern California, there would be none of the racism he encountered daily in his home of New York City. He was highly confident in his basketball abilities and felt that Coach Wooden, who had just won the first two of what would become his record ten National Championships, would be a good coach to help him achieve his basketball dreams. He had no idea of the ultimate impact their more than fifty-year relationship would have upon him as a human being.

His very first meeting in Wooden's little office surprised young Alcindor. As he looked back on the friendship they would build over their lifetimes, this first meeting should have given him a clue that Wooden's loyalty to him as a human being would be the guiding principle in building their lasting bond. In that first meeting, Coach Wooden didn't say one single word about basketball. Their entire conversation was about academics and family. And over the course of their relationship, those two cornerstones would always come first.

It didn't take long for Alcindor to discover that his belief that racism would not follow him to Los Angeles was tremendously naïve. Everywhere he went with the UCLA team throughout what was then the Pacific 8 Conference, Alcindor (who would ultimately convert to Islam in 1968 and adopt the name Kareem Abdul-Jabbar in 1971) was blistered with racial epithets and attacked viciously as a freak and sub-human. It was not until much later in life that Jabbar learned how this cruel treatment and racism had shaken Coach Wooden and deepened his loyalty and compassion for Kareem and for every person of color.

In 1968, Kareem chose to not play for the United States in the Olympic Games because of his convictions about racial injustice and inequality. Coach Wooden received a letter from a woman who was highly critical of Kareem and of himself. Only after Coach Wooden's death more than forty years later did Kareem read a copy of the letter Wooden had written to the woman. In his letter, Wooden defended Kareem and complimented his character, courage, and willingness to stand up for his beliefs. Coach Wooden never said a word about this letter to Kareem. He believed that true loyalty is expressed through actions more than words. He wasn't loyal so that he would receive credit or anything in return. Instead, simply being loyal to the people for whom he cared and doing what he felt was right was reward enough.

Years after Coach Wooden passed away, Kareem learned of another example of the depth of Wooden's loyalty. Before he came to UCLA, Wooden coached at Indiana State University. His teams did very well and received an invitation to the NAIA Championships that would be held in Kansas City. However, the invitation carried with it a condition. The Indiana State team included a black player named Clarence Walker. When the NAIA reached out to invite Indiana State, they stipulated that Wooden was not to bring Walker to the tournament.

Without hesitation, Wooden calmly and clearly turned down the invitation and explained that Clarence Walker was as much a part of that team as any other player. If he was not allowed to participate in the tournament, Indiana State would not do so either. The following year, Wooden's Indiana State team performed even better. Once again, the invitation to play in the NAIA Championships was extended. Before Coach Wooden could refuse the invitation (since Clarence was still a member of the team), the NAIA representative told Wooden that the rule had been changed and the whole squad would be able to participate in the tournament. Coach Wooden's loyalty to Clarence Walker (who incidentally had never even been a starter), to his team, and most of all to his principles and beliefs, had ignited real change.

Once again, Jabbar was stunned and moved by this story. It was a definitive moment in the civil rights movement nearly twenty years before the time of Martin Luther King and the great demonstrations of the '60s. As Jabbar thought back to his time at UCLA, he reflected about how impressed he would have been to know this story. He realized that many coaches would have boasted about it and tried to use the story to win points with their players of color. But, once again, Coach Wooden never said a word. Loyalty was not about scoring points to Coach Wooden. Loyalty was about honor, integrity, and humanity.

The third of Coach Wooden's *Pyramid of Success* foundational blocks expressed his solid belief that we are at our best when we are interdependent rather than independent. True cooperation means that everyone is giving their best effort so that everyone benefits. This is a very important distinction because some people think that to cooperate you must give up some of your talents and gifts so that others can reap the rewards. But it was clear to John Wooden that when everyone cooperated, everyone improved, elevated their performance, and received the maximum benefit.

To cooperate and build a high-performance team everyone must learn to value and honor differences.

Coach Wooden often used the analogy of an automobile to describe a beautifully running team. When he had superstars on his team like Kareem Abdul Jabbar and Bill Walton, they were like the engine. But an engine doesn't get you anywhere without wheels. The players who did the little things, the dirty work like playing aggressive defense, setting screens, and diving for loose balls, were the wheels that enabled the engine to move everyone forward. Players who rarely saw action in the games but challenged their teammates every day in practice were like the lug nuts that kept the wheels from falling off. When there is cooperation, everyone is important and makes a difference.

These three people-centered blocks at the foundation of the Pyramid, friendship, loyalty, and cooperation, are bound together by one essential ingredient: Being fully present. When we are fully present, we send a clear message to those around us that they are important and significant. That is our most vital job as leaders, teachers, and parents. When people know they are important, they rise. When they feel insignificant or unimportant, they fall.

In every single moment I spent with Coach Wooden, whether in person or on the phone, I sensed his full presence. When we were together, he made me feel as if nothing was more important to him than our interaction. It was stunning to me that the all-time greatest men's college basketball coach, one of the greatest leaders of our time, was so fully present with everyone he encountered. His interest in people was unmistakable because he was completely genuine and sincere.

I always left those conversations with Coach Wooden feeling inspired that I could make a real difference in this world. He had the same profound impact on virtually everyone he knew because he so consistently exercised his self-control by letting go of the past, not worrying about the future, and recognizing that the gift is now and that is why they call it the present.

17.

SELF-CONTROL

Coach Wooden believed that only by focusing persistently on the things you do control and letting go of those you don't, can you approach your potential and achieve mastery. This was his constant message to his players, both through words and example. That is why in his twenty-seven years at UCLA he never said the words *winning* or *losing* to his players. Did he want to win? Absolutely! But what he wanted much more was for his players to concentrate on what was most crucial to control: Their effort, energy, attitude, team focus, and presence.

When you maintain self-control during the toughest times, you send an unmistakable message to others to maintain faith, enthusiasm, and focus. You recognize that the most important role of a coach, teacher, parent, or leader is to be an example. True leaders are an example of confidence and centeredness in the midst of adversity and uncertainty. Through a proven phenomenon known as the Pygmalion Effect, which explains that your thoughts and expectations are magnetic, actually pulling others in the direction of those thoughts and expectations, you can breathe positive belief into those around you.

With self-control, we put ourselves at the cause of our experiences and emotions rather than at the effect. We recognize that though we do not control our genetics (abilities, mental acuity, and innate talent), we do control our choices and actions to develop them.

Through self-control, you can disagree with someone without being disagreeable. This was one of Coach Wooden's most important lessons to his players about working as a team. Just as in business, families, relationships, and life, communication is pivotal on the basketball court. You must be able to respond swiftly and flexibly to suggestions, direction, and corrections without becoming angry, frustrated, or hurt. It is through self-control that you can both give and receive communication constructively rather than destructively.

Self-control provides the bricks and mortar from which personal responsibility is built. When you exemplify self-control, you embrace the empowering belief that if things are to change, you must change.

In June of 2016, the then First Lady, Michelle Obama, was interviewed by Oprah Winfrey at the first official United State of Women Summit in Washington, D.C. The timing of this summit was almost providential, for the great Coach Pat Summitt, who had such an enormous impact on elevating women in our society, passed away that same month. The summit's purpose was to bring together women from all over the nation to talk openly about significant gender and equality issues and to generate solutions and strategies to ignite genuine progress.

In her interview with Oprah, the then First Lady focused on the paramount importance of developing self-esteem. And, at the very core of self-esteem, she said, is self-control. Women of great influence such as Michelle Obama, Oprah, and Pat Summitt, though revered and admired by many, are also the constant targets of merciless criticism and scrutiny. As they open new doors and break through old glass ceilings, inspiring new generations of young people along the way, they also stir up great resentment and animosity. Others often wish to keep them from disrupting the status quo and challenging past inequalities and ways of thinking.

Michelle told the room of mesmerized young women that only through self-control and focus on their decisions and actions can they build lasting self-esteem. She encouraged these young women to give no energy to mean-spirited attacks and gossip over which they have no control, to let go of the crippling need for external approval, and to focus instead on doing something each day of great consequence that they care deeply about.

In her June 2016 interview with Oprah Winfrey, Michelle said, "Let those actions speak for themselves. That would shut up the haters, because I would have a whole portfolio of stuff that defined me because it's what I did and not what you called me. The best revenge is success and good work."

As the great motivational speaker Jim Rohn said, "It's not what happens, it's what you DO that makes the difference." And

John Wooden's hero, Mother Theresa, took that truth one step further when she said, "It's not just what you do that matters. It's the love you put into the doing." Self-control is about living according to your values and making your choices and actions love-centered rather than fear-based. No one exercised self-control better than John Wooden.

18.

ALERTNESS

On one of my visits to Coach Wooden he told me, "There are no overachievers. We are all under-achievers. We have more potential than we can imagine." The more I digested this wisdom, the more I realized that there is perhaps no other block in his Pyramid where we have greater under-used capacity than Alertness. Rarely do we fully use our ability to truly take in all that is happening in our world.

For more than twenty years I have asked the participants in my seminars this question: What color is a yield sign? And for more than twenty years every single one of the more than 1,800 audiences I've spoken to have overwhelmingly answered, "Yellow."

Over forty years ago the United States converted to the International Signage Standards. And every yield sign you've seen through all those years is not yellow. Every single one is red and white.

You've seen thousands of yield signs. You see the same ones every day as you drive to work, school, or home. And you haven't seen one of them as it actually is. So, here's the big question—why? Why don't you see them when they're right there in front of you?

The answer reveals the great opportunity we have to develop our alertness. You see, we rarely use our vision to see. Instead, we use our memory and our conditioning. And whenever we use our memory to see, we do not see what *is*. We see what *was*. And the moment we lock on to what was, guess what we block out? We close off what *is* and what *could be*.

Where did Coach Wooden believe it most valuable to turn up our alertness, to actually use our vision to see? The answer is one word—people. Change the way you look at people and the people you look at change. Change the way you see yourself and the self you see will change.

What an enormous difference turning up your alertness can make in your understanding, appreciation, and relationships with others! As you develop your alertness you become aware of more and more opportunities to help those around you grow and thrive. You become a true servant leader.

When Dick Vitale started as a high school hoops coach in 1974, he wrote to some of the coaches he admired most for words of advice. He was stunned when one of the few who wrote back to him was John Wooden. Vitale could hardly believe that someone of Wooden's stature would take the time to offer advice to, in Vitale's words, a nobody. Coach Wooden's advice was simple and clear. "Be organized, make things simple, and have within you that enthusiasm to set the tone."

A few years later Wooden announced a game at which Vitale was coaching. Thanks to his keen alertness, Coach Wooden noticed the exceptional energy and enthusiasm poured into Vitale's coaching. Not long after, Coach Wooden recommended Dick Vitale as someone he thought would make a terrific basketball announcer or commentator to a producer at a brand-new television network called ESPN. Dickie V got his tryout and the rest is history.

Vitale expressed his heartfelt personal tribute this way, "Coach Wooden's legacy is winner, winner, winner in every way of life. Not just winning basketball games, but building men and building character. He did it far beyond his own team roster, though. He did it for a nobody high school coach who wrote to him for advice, and who he later figured deserved a shot at sharing his enthusiasm for the game in a new way." Thanks to John Wooden's alertness, one of the game's greatest ambassadors has been able to share his unique passion and style with millions of college basketball fans for over forty years.

Coach Wooden's wisdom about alertness hit me, very personally, like a lightning bolt when my oldest daughter, Kelsey, came home the first time from college for Thanksgiving break. I finally realized how long I had been seeing her as if she was an old yellow yield sign. Though I adore her, I'd been looking at her as if she was still my little eleven-year-old girl.

She'd been driving her own car for three years! Every day she was waking up hundreds of miles away from us and deciding for herself what she was going to do with the greatest gift we are ever given, called today. She walked in the door that Thanksgiving and announced to my wife Carole and me that she had already applied for and already been accepted to go to a very special program in Africa. My daughter wants to make the world better.

I looked at my Kelsey that day, maybe for the very first time. I finally understood the truth that Coach Wooden tried to teach everyone he knew. Every time I looked at Kelsey like she was still a little girl, every time I used my memory instead of my alertness and vision to see her as if she was an old yellow yield sign, what happened to our relationship? It went *backward* until I looked at the wise, courageous, mature, and incredible young woman who was standing right in front of me. When you truly turn up your alertness you become a world-class yield sign finder!

If we underuse our vision, it pales when we consider how much more we could develop our listening. When we're in a conversation, what are we doing in our minds as the others are speaking? Most of us, if perfectly honest, would have to admit that as others are talking we're formulating our responses. In other words, we're not fully listening to them, we're actually listening to ourselves, our own self-talk. And today, with the proliferation of technology, we're listening to one another even less as we retreat into our tablets and cell phones.

John Wooden, like Pat Summitt, was an extraordinary listener. Like one of his heroes, St. Francis of Assisi, he sought first to understand before seeking to be understood. He often said the good Lord was very wise when he gave us two ears and only one mouth. We would do well to keep that ratio in mind. This was one of Coach Wooden's greatest strengths and secrets to his remarkable success as a teacher and coach.

The most powerful secret to enhance learning is to develop alertness. It requires humility and genuine respect for others to become committed to this block of the Pyramid, for you must believe that there is always more to discover from every experience and interaction. Sometimes the greatest obstacle to discovering the truth is the belief that you already know it. When you turn up your alertness you will never stop learning. For both John Wooden and Pat Summitt, this was a championship secret!

19.

INITIATIVE

There is a substantial difference between knowing what to do and doing what you know. To truly walk your talk requires you to develop the block of the Pyramid Coach Wooden dubbed Initiative.

To John Wooden, to demonstrate initiative meant living your life and exercising your choices proactively rather than reactively. So often we can become paralyzed by the fear of failure. In sports this has often been described as playing "not to lose." With this mindset, tightness replaces flow, instinct and freedom of movement are overwhelmed by caution and feelings of heaviness, restriction, and indecision.

Initiative is born of enthusiasm. When you exercise initiative, you act from the "want to, choose to, love to" perspective rather than the "have to or else" motivation. Initiative is faith rather than fear-based. Wooden often said, "Do not let what you cannot do interfere with what you can do."

When you exercise initiative, you affirm that your energy is your choice. You take ownership of your energy. Coach Wooden knew that people remember relatively little of what you say, no matter how well you say it. But they never forget your energy. Because of this, he knew that in essence, his energy was his example.

At the beginning of each season, Coach Wooden instructed his players in great detail on the proper way to put on their shoes and socks. Most of the players' initial reactions were of amazed disbelief. Did he really believe they didn't know how to put on their shoes and socks? Was it really such a big deal? What had they gotten themselves into?

But over time, as they came to really know John Wooden, they began to understand. His extraordinary attention to detail was actually a vivid demonstration of a level of energy and initiative about the importance of details and thinking ahead that only the greatest teachers and leaders grasp. Wooden told them, "Basketball is a game played on a hardwood floor. To be good, you have to change your direction, change your pace. That's hard on your feet. Your feet are very important as a basketball player. So, if you don't have every wrinkle out of your sock you'll develop blisters. The pain you feel from those blisters may cause you to compensate and to become out of balance as you run and jump. That could lead to a serious injury to your knees or ankles."

Wooden's "sock symposium" helped his players develop that same level of initiative, self-discipline, focus, and meticulous preparation he knew led to true excellence.

Most of all, initiative requires courage to overcome the fear of failure driven by the need for approval. Coach Wooden was known for calling very few time-outs during "crunch time," the often pivotal final five minutes of each half of play. What's more, just like Pat Summitt, he always considered his most important coaching and teaching to take place in daily practices rather than games.

Both of these unusual methods were the result of his conscious desire to ignite initiative and inspire his players to move from fear to freedom…from failure to faith. He did not want his players looking for guidance over their shoulders at him on the bench in crucial moments. He wanted them to move proactively and freely with the unconscious competence they had developed through their training.

A secret Coach Wooden employed to develop initiative in his players was found in the way he viewed discipline. To John Wooden, discipline was used to teach, correct, and improve, never to punish. He developed the sandwich method for correcting mistakes. When players made errors, he first showed them the correct action or decision. He then clearly demonstrated or explained what the player had actually done. Finally, he once again taught them the correct action and decision. Using this two-to-one ratio (correct action—actual action/mistake—correct action) was a practical and effective application of his determined focus on learning from mistakes rather than dwelling on them. It was a subtle yet powerful way to support his definition of success: "Success is peace of mind from knowing you've done the best of which you're capable." And it was a highly effective way to ignite initiative, which is a vital step to achieve competitive greatness.

Perhaps the most important application of Initiative to John Wooden was in dedication to becoming a lifelong learner. He said, "Five years from now, you're the same person except for the people you've met and the books you've read." His admiration for those who exercised initiative was the reason he welcomed so many people into his home when they reached out to him because they wanted to talk with him, learn from him, or interview him. He wanted to reward their initiative, desire to learn, and courage. Because of his great humility, he also deeply believed that there was something to learn from every person and every interaction.

As a coach, Wooden exercised initiative in a very powerful and effective way. Each off-season, he dedicated himself to the study of some specific aspect of basketball. In the early years his focus tended to be more on physical elements of the game like rebounding or defensive positioning. Later, he zeroed in on some more mental and psychological topics like visualization.

He spent the entire off-season digging into his chosen topic with relentless initiative. He read absolutely everything he could on the topic. He identified other coaches or professionals who had great expertise in that area and interviewed them or attended their workshops and lectures. Before his new season began, he organized and synthesized the extensive information he had gathered into a clear composite. He then used this throughout the year to elevate his team's performance in that aspect of the game.

"The Great One" from ice hockey, Wayne Gretzky said, "I've missed 100% of the shots I never took." The truth is, you may not make the shot. But only with initiative will you take the shot. And when it's all said and done, you won't regret the shots you took and missed. You'll regret the shots you could have taken but chose fear over faith.

20.

INTENTNESS

As with most everything he did, based upon careful consideration and common sense, John Wooden chose to place the Intentness and Initiative blocks of his Pyramid side by side. Initiative is about overcoming the fear of failure so you can act with energy and flexibility. Intentness is all about keeping at it with purpose and persistence. Coach Wooden chose the word intentness for this block, rather than persistence or perseverance, to align those qualities with the power of purpose. Persistence without clear purpose can lead to stubbornly doing the same thing over and over again and expecting a different result. With intentness, you operate with the desired end always in mind.

When driving your car to your destination, if you stubbornly latch on to the steering wheel and refuse to adjust to what's in front of you, you'll end up in a ditch. With intentness you remain determined to reach your destination, but become flexible and creative in your approach.

Before Coach Wooden began his unprecedented run of ten National Championships in twelve years, he was known as a good coach who just couldn't seem to win the big one. It was the combination of his intentness and initiative that first enabled him to keep those outside comments in perspective, and ultimately led him to make subtle, conscious changes and adjustments. This resulted in UCLA's historic performance. Coach Wooden knew that within every adversity is planted the seed of equivalent or greater benefit. His intentness ignited him to look for the benefit and learn from the adversity. His initiative led him to take new action in the direction of his intended destination.

It is very important to remember that John Wooden's ultimate goal was not to win National Championships. Of course, he wanted to accomplish that exciting result and he was very proud of those achievements. But his constant and higher intent, both for himself and his teams, was to achieve his definition of success through applying the lessons of the Pyramid: "To attain peace of mind that is a direct result of self-satisfaction in knowing you gave your best effort to become the best of which you are capable."

This intentness kept him focused on what he could control, not on what he couldn't. He could not control the opposing team or if UCLA won or lost the game. He *could* control his effort to reach his potential and teach his players to strive for the same. To John Wooden becoming *the* best was only possible by the constant intent on becoming *your* best.

Coach Wooden understood that when you live with intentness, you fill each day with meaning. When your life is filled with meaning, you seem to radiate joy and positivity. Getting things done becomes inspiring, satisfying, and immensely fun. Intentness ignites your passion for learning. Two tremendous examples of this kind of intentness are Bill and Melinda Gates.

In 2010 they started The Giving Pledge, along with Warren Buffett, where they promised to give away the vast majority of their fortunes to charities and causes for which they held great passion. Long before they formally announced the Pledge, they had already immersed themselves in this work through the Bill and Melinda Gates Foundation. Their intentness to dramatically improve healthcare worldwide, eradicate diseases such as polio, HIV, tuberculosis, and malaria in less developed countries, fight poverty, and elevate the quality of education in rural America, filled them both with unstoppable energy.

In their Foundation's Annual Letter, Bill Gates expressed the enormous happiness and constant internal motivation that comes from intentness when he wrote, "At Microsoft, I got deep into computer science. At the Foundation, it's computer science plus biology, chemistry, agronomy, and more. I'll spend hours talking to a crop researcher or an HIV expert, and then I'll go home, dying to tell Melinda what I've learned."

Coach Wooden sought to help every player he ever coached to develop this kind of intentness, for he always believed he coached people first and basketball second. One of the greatest sources of pride in his life was what his former players went on to accomplish in theirs. He said, "I'm extremely proud of the fact that almost all of the players I had under my supervision have done well in whatever profession they chose. I'm more proud of that than the fact that I had players who were able to win a number of national championships."

21.

CONDITION

Talent without conditioning is unrealized potential. Just as Pat Summitt taught that it is crucial to not only work hard, but also to work smart, Coach Wooden emphasized that industriousness is only truly valuable when you condition the right habits, actions, and beliefs. Most of all, he believed that only through balanced conditioning—physical, mental, emotional, and spiritual—can we approach our potential.

Virtually everyone who knew him never met anyone who exemplified balanced conditioning as much as John Wooden. When it comes to mental conditioning, most of us rarely, if ever, consciously express and affirm our foundational beliefs. Coach Wooden did this every single day by repeating his "Woodenisms." These were short, powerful statements of his principles and philosophy communicated through his daily recitation of poetry and through his practice of focusing on his Seven Point Creed. This creed was given to him by his father when he was eight-years-old.

John Wooden always kept a copy of it with him as a foundation of his conditioning. The Pyramid itself gave him a powerful structure to condition himself and those around him through his teaching and coaching. As a result, the lessons from each block of the Pyramid were given fresh life every day. They stayed top of mind because he applied them and taught them consistently. Pat Summitt used her Definite Dozen in the same way.

Coach Wooden stayed physically fit and active into his nineties. Throughout his career at UCLA, he walked five miles every morning before he designed each day's practice and exercised moderation in his diet and health habits. He believed deeply that conditioning a healthy lifestyle strengthened his spirit and ability to deal with challenges. His UCLA teams were renowned for their full court press, which required an extraordinary level of physical conditioning. Coach Wooden's practices were accordingly filled with constant, focused movement and physical conditioning. He believed strongly that this was a key to UCLA's uncanny consistency in playing their best in the final minutes of games and as the seasons reached their climaxes at the NCAA Tournament. Conditioning was the ultimate secret to constant improvement.

Warren Buffett, the financial guru and single-most successful investor in America, learned a powerful secret about conditioning from John Wooden. He has applied it throughout his over fifty-year career.

The conventional basketball wisdom of the day was that it was important to rest your starters periodically during games so there would always be fresh players on the court. What's more, the prevailing belief at the time was that by giving minutes to the players at the end of your bench who were quite often younger and less experienced, you were preparing the team for future years as they became juniors and seniors. (This was well before the one and done world of college basketball we see today). So, most coaches used a nine to twelve player rotation going deep into the bench.

Coach Wooden eschewed that approach and instead, played his top seven players almost exclusively. There were two fundamental reasons why Wooden used this unorthodox and innovative strategy. First and foremost, he felt that by playing his best players, his opponents would never have the advantage of focusing on attacking less experienced or talented players. He was emphasizing strengths rather than trying to manage around weaknesses. Basketball is a game of runs. Wooden observed that many times big runs would start when coaches sent their second units onto the floor, but would often continue when starters returned. This was due to the opponent gaining confidence and momentum that carried over when the stars came back off the bench.

Second, Coach Wooden believed that by playing his starters and rotating in his top two reserves, those seven would develop superior conditioning and enhance their skills, chemistry, and confidence. Though Wooden used this seven-man rotation, he continually sought to emphasize to his other players who saw very few minutes on the court how important their contributions, efforts, and attitudes were to the team every day in practice. He was direct and honest with every single player about his system of playing only the top seven. His reserves knew what they had signed up for. And they also knew that by working to get better and demonstrating great attitudes, they always had a fair chance to crack that top seven.

Charlie Munger, the long-time friend and partner of Warren Buffett who served as Vice Chairman of Berkshire Hathaway, explained Buffet's application of this lesson this way:

"Buffett out-Woodened Wooden, because the exercise of skill was concentrated in one person (himself), not seven, and his skill improved as he got older during fifty years, instead of deteriorating like the skill of a basketball player does. Moreover, by concentrating so much power and authority in the often-long-serving CEOs of important subsidiaries, Buffett was also creating strong, Wooden-type effects there. Such effects enhanced the skills of the CEOs and the achievements of the subsidiaries. Then, as the Berkshire system bestowed much desired autonomy on many subsidiaries and their CEOs, and Berkshire became successful and well-known, these outcomes attracted both more and better subsidiaries into Berkshire, and better CEOs as well. These better subsidiaries and CEOs then required less attention from headquarters, creating what is often called a 'virtuous cycle.'"

In the same way, Coach Wooden's approach built so much trust among his top seven that both he and they believed they were ready to be at their best when the games were on the line.

Spiritually, Coach Wooden was a very devout Christian. However, like his hero Mother Theresa, he never sought to impose his religious beliefs on others. He was extremely accepting and tolerant of others. He felt the most powerful way to express his spiritual conditioning was simply to walk his talk and live with gratitude, humility, kindness, and love. He did not try to tell others what to believe spiritually, but encouraged them to believe. Again, without spiritual conditioning, reaching one's potential was simply not possible in John Wooden's eyes.

Two words meant more to John Wooden than any others: Thank you. He felt that any day in which we did not express gratitude by voicing those two simple, yet remarkably important words, was a day we left empty. He sought to condition appreciation for others into his players, children, and coaches because he believed that, "Individually we may be many, but only together can we be much."

Synergy and teamwork depended on unselfishness and gratitude for one another's efforts. In the spirit of Pat Summitt's Definite Dozen principle (putting the team before yourself), if Wooden's players failed to give a nod or a thank you to teammates for setting good screens, making good passes, or helping on defense, the bench would become their immediate destination.

22.

SKILL

I t is no coincidence that Coach Wooden placed the Skill block at the very center, and therefore the heart, of his Pyramid. Developing skill requires the relentless, determined effort and repetition represented by the blocks that support it on the Industriousness side of the Pyramid: Industriousness, Self-Control, and Condition.

But that is not enough to develop extraordinary skill. For this we need equal focus and passion on the Enthusiasm side of the Pyramid leading to the Skill block: Enthusiasm, Intentness, and Team Spirit. Without these blocks to balance the three on the Industriousness side, hard work can become tedious and burdensome, leading to burnout.

Finally, the two blocks directly below Skill on the Pyramid

provide the focus and energy needed to work, as Pat Summitt called it, smart, not just hard. Alertness is crucial to the development of skill because without it we can easily fall into the abyss of doing the same thing over and over and over again, and expecting a different result. Alertness ignites us to pay attention to our efforts and ask that vital question, "Is this working?" And then, with initiative, we become inspired to change and try something different.

So, Skill brings together heart, mind, and body. It allows you to love the process of continuous improvement. No matter how hard you work, without truly loving what you do, you'll place a limit on your skill level. That is why the greatest champions from every field of endeavor are as respected and revered for their work ethic as their talent. From sports, John Wooden, Pat Summitt, LeBron James, Michael Jordan, Peyton Manning, Katie Ledecky, Serena Williams, and Tom Brady. From the business arena, Warren Buffett, Mary Barra of GM, Marilyn Hewson of Lockheed Martin, and Jeff Bezos of Amazon. From the world of arts and entertainment, Oprah Winfrey, Tom Hanks, Stephen Spielberg, J.K. Rowling, and Meryl Streep. They exemplify the skill that can be attained when you combine industriousness and enthusiasm, determination and passion.

There are four foundational skills that are most important to develop no matter what field you are in. The first is flexibility. John Wooden's entire Pyramid of Success is built upon controlling what you can control. He believed deeply that you have the capacity to grow in every one of the blocks of the Pyramid, but to do so, you must be flexible in your approach. In a world of rapidly accelerating technological advancement and mindboggling increases in the speed and availability of information, it is essential to live by the belief that if *things* are to change, *you* must change. When you develop the skill of flexibility you become eager to adapt, innovate, and take good risks. You become a "change-thriver."

As focused and structured as he was in his approach to practice sessions, he was a master of flexibility when it came to using his alertness to find ways to improve. When UCLA broke through and won their first championship, Coach Wooden felt that his small change of slightly reducing the intensity of practices as the season wore on provided the spark that had been missing. He saw his players feeling fresher and more energized in the NCAA Tournament as a result of this subtle adjustment. It was Coach Wooden's flexibility that ignited him to keep learning, adapting, and improving.

The second crucial skill to develop for mastery is visualization on the desired outcome. This second master skill is based upon the conviction that what we focus on is what we create. And since what we focus on is what we create, the crucial question becomes: What are we focusing on? How many of us center much of our focus on worrying about what has not yet happened? How often do we lock on to what could go wrong more than what could go right?

Most of us are almost hypnotically drawn to the obstacles, barriers, and weaknesses that block our path to our goals and aspirations. As we develop the master skill of visualization on the desired outcomes, we refocus our energy, talent, passion, and innovativeness on creating what we want. That powerful shift moves us from reaction to proaction, from hesitancy and defensiveness, to faith and positive motion.

The third skill essential to develop personal mastery is quickness in executing fundamentals. As Coach Wooden often said, "Be quick, but never hurry." Quickness comes from focused repetition. Over time, this concentrated attention to detail leads to conscious competence. True skill, however, requires that you go one step further with your detailed repetition of fundamentals. You must move beyond conscious competence to unconscious competence.

In sport, this is sometimes called the flow, where muscle memory takes over and the athlete performs with peak efficiency as if on a perfectly tuned automatic pilot. While in this state, conscious thought actually disrupts the flow. If you really want to test this, ask a golfer just as they are about to tee off, "Do you breathe in or out on your backswing?" Then watch as their ball flies straight into the water!

Coach Wooden understood that you cannot alter your genetic makeup, your height, or your natural athletic or academic talent. But he believed wholeheartedly that you could improve your quickness in utilizing the talent you have. Developing this third master skill is key to achieving Coach Wooden's definition of success: Becoming the best of which you're capable.

The fourth foundational skill Coach Wooden believed was pivotal in both reaching your own potential and helping others reach theirs, was that transformational secret called *listening*. In 2008, the recipient of the first UCLA Anderson School of Management Global Leadership Award was Starbucks founder and Chairman, Howard Schultz. The ceremony that night was to be an experience that both Schultz and the emcee for the festivities that night, Andy Serwer, Managing Editor of *Fortune Magazine*, would always remember. But it wasn't the excitement of the star-studded crowd at the Beverly Hilton, or even the tremendous honor of being the recipient and presenter of the prestigious award, that would cement that experience into the hearts of these two extraordinarily successful business executives. No, the lasting impact and magic of the evening came from the simple wisdom they received from Coach Wooden and the example of the remarkable skill of listening he had developed over his ninety-seven years.

Before the actual ceremony, Schultz, Serwer, and Wooden gathered for fifteen or twenty minutes in the green room, waiting for their call to the stage. Serwer recalled afterward that he and Howard did pretty much all of the talking. Coach Wooden sat quietly, answering questions politely, yet quite briefly, when asked. Serwer was to begin the program with a one-on-one interview with Coach Wooden, to be followed by a three-party discussion from the stage, at which time Howard was to join them.

Based upon the time they had spent together in the green room, Serwer had become genuinely worried that the interview on stage with Coach Wooden might prove difficult and even uncomfortable. Wooden was a legend, yet he was ninety-seven-years-old. Perhaps time had finally caught up with him, slowing his conversational energy to a crawl. Both Serwer and Schultz were about to learn about the tremendous value of seeking first to understand rather than to be understood.

When they went on stage for the interview, Coach astounded Serwer with the brilliance, wit, and depth of his answers. In reply to Serwer's question about why more people aren't better leaders, Coach explained that too few of us actually listen to those around us. They had not developed the skill. He recited poetry he had learned as a boy to perfectly illustrate the principle. "A wise old owl sat in an oak. The more he heard, the less he spoke. The less he spoke, the more he heard. The more he heard, the more he learned. Now wasn't he a wise old bird."

The entire audience was enthralled, mesmerized, wanting to soak in every ounce of his unparalleled wisdom. When Howard Schultz joined them on stage his first comment was that he almost didn't want to come out to receive the award, but instead to simply stay there in the green room watching the television monitor and listening to every word Coach said.

You see, while Andy Serwer and Howard Schultz had thought that Coach Wooden was simply quiet and reserved as a result of their time together in the green room, he was actually doing what so few of us ever really do…listening. He wanted to know all he could about the two remarkable men he was about to connect with onstage. The master skill he had developed over a lifetime was to listen fully, without formulating a response in his head while the others were speaking. This was his secret: To listen with his heart and mind and not just his ears.

That night, Howard Schultz received a very special and well-earned award as a remarkable Global Leader who had impacted millions while creating a business culture based upon quality, service, and caring about your team. Andy Serwer received the honor of representing *Fortune Magazine* and their passion for developing and publicizing outstanding global leadership.

But the greatest gift they received that night was the lesson they learned from a true master of the power of listening. It is a master skill that will elevate your business, your family, and your life! As John Wooden said so simply, yet powerfully, "Listen if you want to be heard."

23.

TEAM SPIRIT

To John Wooden, Team Spirit was built on one simple but immensely important principle—genuine consideration for others. This meant, "Complete eagerness to lose oneself in the team, for the good of the team." When you come from the place of genuine consideration for others, you are able to disagree without being disagreeable and move beyond defensiveness. When it comes to working with others, this is the secret to replacing destruction with construction.

At the heart of true consideration for others is unselfishness. With this unselfish foundation for Team Spirit, your absolute determination to never let your teammates down is a far higher priority than personal glory or gain. Wooden said, "Consider the rights of others before your own feelings, and the feelings of others before your own rights."

When it came to recruiting players to UCLA, Coach Wooden looked for one attribute more than any other: A burning desire to reach one's potential, but always in relation to the team. He wanted players who prized team accomplishments far above individual ones. When you think of the many great players he coached, from 5'10" Gail Goodrich, to 6'11" Bill Walton, and 7'1" Kareem Abdul Jabbar, Wooden's stars embodied unselfishness. They always looked to pass if a teammate had a better shot, to play full out on defense, and to give credit for their own achievements to their coaches and teammates.

Coach Wooden built upon this unselfish spirit by using his alertness to recognize and commend those who didn't get a lot of press and whose contributions didn't show up on the stat sheet. He commended team members for the little things that sometimes made the biggest difference, like diving for loose balls, setting rock solid screens, and challenging the stars to work harder every day in practice.

Most of all, John Wooden believed the only way to teach Team Spirit was to be a constant example of genuine consideration for others. When you were with John Wooden he gave you his undivided attention and focus. He was completely present. He treated everyone with dignity and respect. When he needed to impose discipline, he did so without animosity or personal attack. He was clear, honest, and no nonsense. And when that discipline was complete, there was no lingering upset or disappointment. There was no probationary period. The lesson had been delivered and it was now time for a fresh start.

In this way, his players understood that the discipline was not aimed at punishing but rather teaching, and that it was always aimed at elevating the team. As he often said, "Individually we may be many, but together we are much."

One of the greatest performances in Olympic history exemplified the almost magical power of Team Spirit. In the 2008 Games in Beijing, the first day of swimming competition was one of the banner events, the men's four by one-hundred-meter freestyle relay.

That night, the American team found itself in an unfamiliar position on the world swimming stage they had dominated for decades. They were heavy underdogs to the French team, led by the world record holder in the one-hundred-meter freestyle, Alain Bernard. In fact, many of the top swimming experts picked the American team to finish third, behind not only the dominant French team, but also a very strong Australian team.

There was added drama attached to the relay because the lead-off swimmer for the Americans was Michael Phelps, whose pursuit of eight gold medals in one Olympics, that would best the all-time record of seven golds won by Mark Spitz in 1972, was the biggest storyline of the entire Games. Unless the Americans somehow pulled of a major upset and won that relay, Phelps' dream would be over after his first individual event.

Bernard, who would go on to win the individual gold medal in the one-hundred-meter freestyle in Beijing, would be swimming the anchor (final) leg of the relay. The American anchorman would be thirty-two-year-old Jason Lezak. Lezak had been a top American sprinter for more than ten years but had never held a world record or won an individual gold medal. Though a seasoned competitor and outstanding relay swimmer, many considered Lezak to be past his prime and not on the same level as Bernard. To put it simply, if the Americans didn't have a substantial lead over the French when Lezak dove in for the final leg, we were in big trouble.

So, when Jason took off from the blocks for the final 100 meters, nearly a body length behind Alain Bernard (and his body was six-foot-five-inches long!) all the world knew the race was over.

But something magical happens in a relay. Team spirit rises to such a level that fear evaporates and your competitor transforms into a source of almost magnetic energy, lifting and pulling you beyond what you thought was possible. All you know is that your team is everything to you, and you feel with absolute certainty that you will not let them down. It's as if they are inside you, giving you the power of four minds, hearts, and bodies combined into one turbo, you.

That's exactly what happened to Jason Lezak that unforgettable night. With less than five meters to go, he had miraculously closed that body-length gap to less than a foot. He was flying, feeling nothing but team energy surging in every one of his sixty trillion cells. Michael Phelps and his relay teammates leaned over the edge of the pool, screaming and cheering at the absolute tops of their lungs, frantically willing Lezak to do the impossible.

The world stopped for a moment as every head spun to look at the electronic scoreboard. A second of stunned silence and then the explosion! The Americans had won the gold by the infinitesimally tiny margin of eight one-hundredths of a second. Jason Lesak had touched out Bernard and swam a time of 46.06, the fastest relay leg ever, and more than a full second faster than the world record.

Ninety-seven-year-old John Wooden watched that relay that night smiling broadly at the remarkable example of team spirit he had just seen. To lose yourself in your team, for the good of the team, is the secret to discovering and unleashing your true potential.

24.

POISE AND CONFIDENCE

In the penultimate level of the Pyramid, Coach Wooden placed two blocks: Poise and Confidence. He saw Poise and Confidence as if they were joined at the hip, two sides to one coin.

Coach Wooden considered Poise as simply being yourself. Poise is all about authenticity and genuineness. When you demonstrate Poise, you are comfortable in your own skin. You don't need others to tell you who you are or to make you feel worthwhile. It is not that you don't have empathy for others, but simply that you are not motivated at all by the need for their approval. As Coach Wooden said, "You can't let praise or criticism get to you. It's a weakness to get caught up in either one."

One of the most important principles that set Coach Wooden apart was his belief that comparing yourself to others was destructive and worthless. He saw the need to compare yourself to others as a powerfully detrimental addiction. When you need others to validate your sense of self, you can never receive enough validation and attention. The momentary lift you might feel from receiving praise or appreciation is swallowed up almost immediately by the irrepressible compulsion that you must receive more. He put it this way, "Never try to be better than someone else. Learn from others, and try to be the best you can be. Success is the by-product of that preparation."

Coach Wooden taught that reaching one's potential was much more a function of we-go than ego. When you are driven by ego, you have an insatiable need to control others. You must be right, must have your way. If not, you feel attacked or belittled. Constructive criticism or suggestions seem like personal affronts. You become the exact opposite of being easy to impress but hard to offend. Instead, you quickly become defensive whenever someone questions you or your position.

With Poise, you can easily laugh at yourself and learn from everyone. Those who disagree with you are not feared as threats but rather as sources of alternative ways of looking at the world. Those who disagree can introduce you to different views but they cannot disturb your peace of mind. Coach Wooden believed little could be learned or gained through anger, but much could be accomplished and enhanced through consideration and openness.

Poise requires true integrity. When you are honest with others and yourself there is very little stress in your heart. You have nothing to hide, no dark secrets to guard, and no need to keep yourself safe from what others think. You stop worrying about trying to be the best and find great satisfaction and peace in the journey to simply become your best.

If Poise is being yourself, confidence is the inner knowing that when you are yourself and others are free to be themselves, everything will work out as it should. So, to be truly confident, you must have belief in others as well as yourself.

Coach Wooden believed that true confidence could only come from focusing on controlling what you could control: Your effort, energy, and attitude. In this way, confidence must be built from your choices and actions rather than from the results. The results simply provide the information and feedback necessary to keep learning and improving.

Only those with genuine confidence are comfortable with admitting when they are wrong or have made mistakes. They do not beat themselves up, blame others, or make excuses. They do not blow achievements out of proportion or become depressed or crushed when they fall short of their objectives. They just keep learning and keep taking the shots. They believe that if things are to change, they must change. They believe that if it's to be, it's up to me. Personal responsibility is a privilege and not a burden when you embody confidence.

True confidence is contagious. It is impervious to external storms and steady as you move between the highest peaks and deepest valleys. It is the opposite of arrogance and boastfulness, which is based upon comparing yourself to others and the need for approval. Confidence is knowing that in every moment and situation you can choose to give the best of which you're capable. You know that everyone around you is fully capable of making that same choice. Confidence is not about beating others. It is about being your best and feeling genuine joy and inner satisfaction that giving your all is enough.

When you are truly confident, you want to win and love to compete, but your self-worth does not depend upon the result. Instead, it depends on the effort and energy you give. You are comfortable giving credit to your competitors and determined to learn and grow from every experience and outcome. Confidence is giving everything you've got to the journey and having complete faith that by doing so, you'll arrive at the destination that is right for you.

Coach Wooden instilled confidence in the way he taught and led. He believed that by focusing on positive actions rather than reactive, defensive ones, his players would emerge with greater confidence. For example, he taught his players that the key to rebounding was to get between their opponent and the ball and then go and get the basketball, rather than worrying about boxing out. In other words, he wanted them to zero in on the positive action of getting the ball that was in front of them instead of looking behind them and focusing on trying to keep their opponent from getting position.

When the NCAA banned the dunk shot as a direct attempt to slow down the dominance of Kareem Abdul Jabbar, Coach Wooden encouraged Kareem to see this as a tremendous opportunity to develop even greater skills and excellence. The result was Kareem's mastery of his sky hook which still stands to this day as the most dominant shot the game has ever seen. This shot played a huge role in Jabbar becoming the all-time leading scorer in NBA history—a record that stood for thirty-four years until broken in 2023 by LeBron James. As Wooden said, "Things work out best for those who make the best of the way things work out."

25.

COMPETITIVE GREATNESS

The reason Coach Wooden chose the Pyramid as the structure for his principles and teaching was his belief that we build toward our potential block by block. This growth starts with the foundation and then interconnects as we rise to the pinnacle of Competitive Greatness. By mastering the lessons of the fourteen blocks that support competitive greatness, we put ourselves in position to become the best of which we're capable.

To Coach Wooden, competitive greatness was not determined by winning or losing or by records and accolades. He viewed competitive greatness as something everyone can attain. Simply put, competitive greatness is being your best when your best is called for. It is not necessarily easy, but it is always available.

It requires industriousness and enthusiasm through friendship, loyalty, and cooperation. It requires self-control, alertness, initiative, and intentness. It requires condition, skill, and team spirit. And finally, it requires poise and confidence. It is not about comparison to others. Instead, it is about giving 100% and making those around you better in the process.

This last point is crucial because Coach Wooden believed that synergy and teamwork led to far greater results than separate individual performance and talent. Once again, the best aspect about human beings is that we will do more for others than we'll do for ourselves. So, it is immensely satisfying to help those around us to rise closer to their Competitive Greatness.

Competitive Greatness begins on the inside and spreads to the outside. It lifts others to believe in themselves and each other. When you achieve Competitive Greatness, you require no external approval, nor do you seek to control others. You are a human catalyst, igniting others through the sheer joy of giving everything you've got with passion and exciting purpose. You give credit and take responsibility. You love complimenting and talking about your teammates but have no need to boast about yourself. With Competitive Greatness you love what you do and do what you love, and that is the perfect recipe for a winning life!

Throughout *Lessons from the Legends*, you have seen incredible examples of Competitive Greatness through true champions stepping forward to give their best when their best is called for.

The Sister Survivors, 140 strong who stood tall together to say to millions that self-respect is more powerful than abuse, and that cover-ups are no match for courage.

LeBron James, whose vision, passion, and determination brought the I Promise School to Akron, Ohio, so that thousands of children will have a far greater chance than ever before to transform from statistics to stars.

Reese Witherspoon, who had the audacity to be ambitious and shake up an entire industry, opening new possibilities for women that will be seen by billions of moviegoers around the globe.

Peyton Manning, who will never stop caring more about children than credit, more about families than fame.

Michael Phelps, whose greatest accomplishment was not his twenty-eight Olympic medals, but rather in moving from fear to freedom and from failure to faith, to be the best husband, father, and example he can be.

Oprah Winfrey, whose irrepressible enthusiasm has led her from poverty and abuse to become perhaps the most influential woman on earth.

And finally, single mothers and grandmothers throughout America and the world, who work two and three jobs, seven days a week to give their children a chance at a better life.

Most of all, you have learned Competitive Greatness from two remarkable human beings, John Wooden and Pat Summitt. These two Coaches of the Century walked their talk and genuinely lived the principles they taught. The time has never been more perfect to focus on these real-life examples of Competitive Greatness. One a man and one a woman, one from the East and one from the West. One all passion and intensity, the other calm and even-keeled. Both of their teaching, foundational principles, and most of all, real-life examples provide a winning game plan to help everyone refocus. Refocus on character rather than reputation, reason over ratings, humility over hype, and excellence over ego.

Not only did Pat Summitt and John Wooden exemplify this extraordinary level of integrity, they proved that it provides a championship formula that generates remarkable results. They believed passionately that it is a formula that is available to everyone. They believed that you have everything you need right now to become a shining light of Competitive Greatness. When you live with this focus over time, as did these two legends, your character will become your reputation.

About The Author

Brian Biro is America's #1 Breakthrough Speaker! He is one of the nation's foremost speakers and teachers of Leadership, Possibility Thinking, Thriving on Change, and Team-Building. He has delivered more than 1,800 presentations around the world in the past thirty years. A major client offered the best introduction about Brian's impact when he said, "Brian Biro has the energy of a ten-year-old, the enthusiasm of a twenty-year-old, and the wisdom of a seventy-five-year-old." A former vice-president of a major transportation corporation, Brian has authored fifteen books, including bestseller, *Beyond*

Success! He graduated with honors from Stanford and served as the President of the UCLA Graduate School of Management Student Association while earning his MBA from UCLA. Brian has appeared on *Good Morning America*, CNN's *Business Unusual*, and has been a guest on more than three-hundred radio programs as well as dozens of podcasts throughout the world. Brian was named one of the UCLA Graduate School of Management's 100 Most Inspirational Graduates in the seventy-five-year history of the school. Most recently, Brian was also honored as one of the top 10 Interactive speakers in North America and one of the top 60 Motivational Speakers in the world.

To contact Brian about speaking for your organization please visit: www.brianbiro.com

A free ebook edition is available with the purchase of this book.

To claim your free ebook edition:

1. Visit MorganJamesBOGO.com
2. Sign your name CLEARLY in the space
3. Complete the form and submit a photo of the entire copyright page
4. You or your friend can download the ebook to your preferred device

Morgan James BOGO™

A **FREE** ebook edition is available for you or a friend with the purchase of this print book.

CLEARLY SIGN YOUR NAME ABOVE

Instructions to claim your free ebook edition:
1. Visit MorganJamesBOGO.com
2. Sign your name CLEARLY in the space above
3. Complete the form and submit a photo of this entire page
4. You or your friend can download the ebook to your preferred device

Print & Digital Together Forever.

Snap a photo

Free ebook

Read anywhere